The Social Network

This in-depth study of one of the twenty-first century's most acclaimed films, *The Social Network: Youth Film 2.0* considers the contribution of David Fincher and Aaron Sorkin's film to the understanding of 'youth' in a contemporary, digital age.

The book starts by situating *The Social Network* within the contexts of 'youth film', arguing that it challenges and reshapes the boundaries of this genre by rethinking the notion of 'youth' itself in the present century. It goes on to consider in detail the aesthetics at work in the film, arguing for its critical and reflexive use of an 'accelerated' audio-visual style, in order to capture both the new visual regimes of the personal computer era, and the ethical and intellectual ambiguities of Facebook itself as a creation. Finally, it locates the film within the broader visual styles and fashion codes of a late twentieth- and early twenty-first-century consumer culture that incorporates and commodifies rebellion and dissent: qualities that underpinned Facebook's emerging, paradoxical identity as at once the epitome of 'hacker' culture and also a multi-billion-dollar global company.

Reframing the meaning of youth cinema, this volume in the Cinema and Youth Culture series is ideal for students, researchers and scholars of cinema studies, youth culture and digital cultures.

Neil Archer is Senior Lecturer in Film at Keele University, UK. He is the author of seven previous books, including *Cinema and Brexit: The Politics of Popular English Film* (2021) and *Twenty-First-Century Hollywood: Rebooting the System* (2019).

Cinema and Youth Cultures
Series Editors: Siân Lincoln and Yannis Tzioumakis

Cinema and Youth Cultures engages with well-known youth films from American cinema as well as the cinemas of other countries. Using a variety of methodological and critical approaches, the series volumes provide informed accounts of how young people have been represented in film, while also exploring the ways in which young people engage with films made for and about them. In doing this, the Cinema and Youth Cultures series contributes to important and long-standing debates about youth cultures, how these are mobilized and articulated in influential film texts and the impact that these texts have had on popular culture at large.

Moonlight
Screening Black Queer Youth
Maria Flood

The Commitments
Youth, Music, and Authenticity in 1990s Ireland
Nessa Johnston

Precious
Identity, Adaptation and the African American Youth Film
Katherine Whitehurst

The Social Network
Youth Film 2.0
Neil Archer

For more information about this series, please visit: https://www. routledge.com/Cinema-and-Youth-Cultures/book-series/CYC

The Social Network
Youth Film 2.0

Neil Archer

Frontispiece The Social Network (2010), courtesy of Moviestore/Shutterstock.

LONDON AND NEW YORK

First published 2022
by Routledge
4 Park Square, Milton Park, Abingdon, Oxon OX14 4RN

and by Routledge
605 Third Avenue, New York, NY 10158

Routledge is an imprint of the Taylor & Francis Group, an informa business

British Library Cataloguing-in-Publication Data
A catalogue record for this book is available from the British Library

Library of Congress Cataloging-in-Publication Data
Names: Archer, Neil, 1971- author.
Title: The social network : youth film 2.0 / Neil Archer.
Description: Abingdon, Oxon ; New York, NY : Routledge, 2022. | Series: Cinema and youth cultures | Includes bibliographical references and index.
Identifiers: LCCN 2021053728 (print) | LCCN 2021053729 (ebook) | ISBN 9780367753108 (hardback) | ISBN 9780367753115 (paperback) | ISBN 9781003161936 (ebook)
Subjects: LCSH: Fincher, David--Criticism and interpretation. | Sorkin, Aaron--Criticism and interpretation. | Social network (Motion picture) | Facebook (Electronic resource) | Youth in motion pictures. | Technology in motion pictures. | Motion pictures--United States--History--21st century.
Classification: LCC PN1997.2.S645 A73 2022 (print) | LCC PN1997.2.S645 (ebook) | DDC 791.43/72--dc23/eng/20220111
LC record available at https://lccn.loc.gov/2021053728
LC ebook record available at https://lccn.loc.gov/2021053729

ISBN: 978-0-367-75310-8 (hbk)
ISBN: 978-0-367-75311-5 (pbk)
ISBN: 978-1-003-16193-6 (ebk)

DOI: 10.4324/9781003161936

Typeset in Times New Roman
by MPS Limited, Dehradun

Contents

Figures

Series Editors' Introduction

Despite the high visibility of youth films in the global media marketplace, especially since the 1980s when Conglomerate Hollywood realized that such films were not only strong box office performers but also the starting point for ancillary sales in other media markets as well as for franchise building, academic studies that focused specifically on such films were slow to materialize. Arguably, the most important factor behind academia's reluctance to engage with youth films was a (then) widespread perception within the Film and Media Studies communities that such films held little cultural value and significance, and therefore were not worthy of serious scholarly research and examination. Just like the young subjects they represented, whose interests and cultural practices have been routinely deemed transitional and transitory, so were the films that represented them perceived as fleeting and easily digestible, destined to be forgotten quickly, as soon as the next youth film arrived in cinema screens a week later.

Under these circumstances, and despite a small number of pioneering studies in the 1980s and early 1990s, the field of 'youth film studies' did not really start blossoming and attracting significant scholarly attention until the 2000s and in combination with similar developments in cognate areas such as 'girl studies'. However, because of the paucity of material in the previous decades, the majority of these new studies in the 2000s focused primarily on charting the field and therefore steered clear of long, in-depth examinations of youth films or was exemplified by edited collections that chose particular films to highlight certain issues to the detriment of others. In other words, despite providing often wonderfully rich accounts of youth cultures as these have been captured by key films, these studies could not have possibly dedicated sufficient space to engage with more than just a few key aspects of youth films.

In more recent (post-2010) years, a number of academic studies started delimiting their focus and therefore providing more space for in-depth examinations of key types of youth films, such as slasher films and biker films, or examining youth films in particular historical periods. From that point on, it was a matter of time for the first publications that focused exclusively on key youth films from a number of perspectives to appear (*Mamma Mia! The Movie*, *Twilight* and *Dirty Dancing* are among the first films to receive this treatment). Conceived primarily as edited collections, these studies provided a multifaceted analysis of these films, focusing on such issues as the politics of representing youth, the stylistic and narrative choices that characterize these films and the extent to which they are representative of a youth cinema, the ways these films address their audiences, the ways youth audiences engage with these films, the films' industrial location and other relevant issues.

It is within this increasingly maturing and expanding academic environment that the Cinema and Youth Cultures volumes arrive, aiming to consolidate existing knowledge, provide new perspectives, apply innovative methodological approaches, offer sustained and in-depth analyses of key films and therefore become the 'go to' resource for students and scholars interested in theoretically informed, authoritative accounts of youth cultures in film. As editors, we have tried to be as inclusive as possible in our selection of key examples of youth films by commissioning volumes on films that span the history of cinema, including the silent film era; that portray contemporary youth cultures as well as ones associated with particular historical periods; that represent examples of mainstream and independent cinema; that originate in American cinema and the cinemas of other nations; that attracted significant critical attention and commercial success during their initial release and that were 'rediscovered' after an unpromising initial critical reception. Together these volumes are going to advance youth film studies while also being able to offer extremely detailed examinations of films that are now considered significant contributions to cinema and our cultural life more broadly.

We hope readers will enjoy the series.

Siân Lincoln & Yannis Tzioumakis
Cinema & Youth Cultures Series Editors

Acknowledgements

My thanks above all to the series editors, Siân Lincoln & Yannis Tzioumakis, for their enthusiasm, encouragement and expertise. Writing this book has been a blast. I'm grateful to both of them for the opportunity.

My love as ever to Giulia and Noa, who have been curious to see what my 'FacebookBook', as they like to call it, is really all about. Well, now you know!

Thanks, finally, to David Fincher and Aaron Sorkin, without whom I would probably still be here, but this book almost certainly wouldn't.

Introduction

Much Too Young – *The Social Network* and Twenty-First-Century Youth Film

'That was the trouble with starting a company when you're under twenty-one. You're underage. You can't drink – but you can start a company'.

(former Atari engineer Al Alcorn, quoted in Fisher 2018: 70)

'They've made a film about *Facebook*?'

This, admittedly, was the thought that went through my mind one summer evening in 2010, when I saw the theatrical trailer for *The Social Network* (Fincher 2010). Like those of the film's various litigants, my memories of the event might be unreliable, but I seem to recall – strangely enough – that it was prior to a screening of *Toy Story 3* (Unkrich 2010). Though eager to discover the fate of Woody and Buzz, I was at that moment less obviously drawn towards a film that chronicled the rise of the world's dominant social media platform. Did we not, after all, know how the story ended? By this point in time, Facebook was being used by one in ten of the world's population, and growing by the year. It did not need any cinematic encouragement. And more to the point, I asked myself – naively, as it turned out – how did Facebook represent a subject for a *movie*?

My initial relationship to *The Social Network* was, then, one of ambivalence. Returning to the trailer now, however, I am reminded just how much this ambivalence towards Facebook, but also *unease* at its implications, is already structured into the publicity for David Fincher and Aaron Sorkin's film.[1] The first forty-five seconds piece together a montage of photographs, the opening one – a young woman, looking over her shoulder, displaying a tattoo – fading up into view through a pixelated screen. We see holiday snaps, a child gymnast on a beam, a baby's feet, girls and boys at a party, couples, and another young woman, looking more anxious than happy, climbing out

DOI: 10.4324/9781003161936-1

of a pool. These are intercut with shots of the Facebook pointing-hand icon, clicking various commands ('Add as a Friend'; 'Confirm'), or of brief comments typed up in extreme close-up ('This day sucks'; 'Where are you?'). Taken out of their context, and cued to Scala's 2002 choral version of Radiohead's 'Creep' – with its lines, echoing over the images, about wanting 'a perfect body' and 'a perfect soul' – the images feel ghostly, drained of human connection. The trailer builds to its concluding tagline, accompanying the dark, also pixelated image of Jesse Eisenberg's unreadable face, his mouth slightly open, poised, at once aggressive and fearful: YOU DON'T GET TO 500 MILLION FRIENDS WITHOUT MAKING A FEW ENEMIES.

This is still a strikingly uneasy, ambiguous message. In an era which has increasingly put a primacy on connectivity, '500 million friends' – a figure that has grown more than fourfold at the time of writing this book – already reinforces a view of Facebook, and maybe even of Mark Zuckerberg, as an agent of *domination*: the same word Facebook's young CEO, just out of his teens, would yell at early company meetings as a way of rallying his workforce (Fisher 2018: 368–70; Levy 2020: 109–10). Yet it also offers an impression of at once extraordinary and hubristic reach. What does 'friend' mean on such a scale? Why would anyone *want* so many friends in the first place – and more to the point, did such a figure not represent something bigger, more disturbing?

The Social Network, after all, was not science fiction, even if it might look that way to a viewer cryogenically frozen before the 1990s. The consequent fact that, by 2010, a story about Facebook seemed potentially banal was the indication in itself of what Facebook had already done to the world. Facebook's ubiquity was one of the reasons I, among others, was unsure about it as a film subject (Kois 2008). Yet the company's unprecedented six-year ascendancy to a form of global domination, as I see it now, is precisely *why* it is such a significant subject for a film: by 2010, it was simply a part of the world in which we were living. Statistically, and especially in the UK or the USA, one would possibly be already among these 500 million 'friends', or at least would be soon enough. As Facebook chronicler Steven Levy has put it, and with no apparent irony, CEO Mark Zuckerberg is not interested in running for political office but is happy to be 'a social theorist with the rare power to affect the communications of 2 billion people. No country on Earth had a population as big as Facebook. The presidency would be a step *down*' (Levy 2020: 383, emphasis in the original).

It was perhaps reasonable of me to feel ambivalent about the prospect of *The Social Network*; though as I will explore in this book, this ambivalence towards its subject is what gives *The Social Network* its peculiar and often unsettling charge. It is probably also wise to note at this point that, while I will acknowledge some of its problematic sides, I am no longer at all ambivalent about Fincher and Sorkin's film. It is still one of the only films whose DVD I purchased the morning it was released, eager to see it again and sift through its several hours of commentary and making-of extras. A version of the same *The Social Network* poster (in Spanish – don't ask me to explain) even hangs on my office wall, staring at me like a kind of warning. Since I am starting this book with full disclosure, and in case any readers are concerned, I should also add that I have no particular trumpet to blow for Zuckerberg's company (I have a placeholder account linked to my film programme's Facebook page: I am not an active user, in spite of Facebook's many encouragements). If I like *The Social Network*, and I really do, it is not because I am enamoured by the products, platforms and creative personnel whose stories the films narrate. Indeed, it is fairly clear from the finished film and its production contexts that *The Social Network* is not a love letter to the Facebook CEO either (Sorkin, in an open letter he later published, highlighted that the main challenge in writing and filming *The Social Network* was '[not to] get sued by Mark Zuckerberg' (Sorkin 2019)). As a 'fan' film, to be sure, it would be a skewed or at best masochistic take on biopic hagiography.

It is nevertheless an interesting aspect of the film's afterlife that for a number of commentators, as I will outline in Chapter 4, *The Social Network* is a film too much enamoured of the young Zuckerberg for its own good. I will argue against this, highlighting that while the film allows for a strong sense of identification with its main protagonist, it also lays bare his many faults. As I also discuss later, one of the challenges in writing about Fincher and Sorkin's film is that it is hard *not* to view it now without our awareness of the later, controversial contexts around Facebook and its CEO. Whatever lustre Facebook once might have had, a decade on from *The Social Network*, most of it has been tarnished by a variety of incidents, misguided statements and scandals. And yet we continue to use Facebook, and continue to let Facebook and its algorithms *use us*, in not significantly diminishing numbers.

Indeed, one of the points highlighted by Brady Robards and Siân Lincoln, in their recent book *Growing Up on Facebook* (2020), is that people, and most significantly *young* people, are still making regular use of Facebook while claiming that it is also not an important part of their lives. When I mentioned to some of my students at Keele that I was writing about *The Social Network*, I asked them whether they saw

Facebook as 'cool'. *Definitely not* seemed to be the shared view. But 'do you use it?' I asked. 'Of course' was the answer. It is a similar view to the one unearthed by Robards and Lincoln, who find not only that the platform has retained its importance to young users, despite its apparent loss of cultural capital, but also that it has shaped so much of the identity, and so many of the memories, of those same young users who have effectively 'grown up on Facebook'.

How that has happened, for good or ill, and how Facebook came to be, is therefore one of the stories of the twenty-first century. More pertinently for this book, though, and for the Cinema and Youth Cultures series for which it is written, it is also a story of *young people* coming of age in this same century. Before going further, though, it is important to stop and think for a moment about some of the contexts around *The Social Network*, and what these might mean for one's understanding of the film, in terms of a cinema about, and for, youth.

'That's Life in the NFL': Sorting the Men from the Boys, and Vice Versa

I was thirty-nine years old when, at the end of 2010, I first saw *The Social Network*. The film, set for the most part in 2003 and 2004, describes a period during which I was in my early thirties, living in the UK, unaware – for a couple more years at least – of an entity called Facebook. In other circumstances, this would be no more than just an anecdotal point. Yet with regard to this book, it is an important acknowledgement of where both I and *The Social Network* are coming from, given the claims I otherwise make for the film as part of a cinema exploring or reflecting the cultures of young people. Evidently, *The Social Network* is not a film either from, or one that speaks directly to, my own youth. To what extent the film itself is about youth at all will be one of this book's main concerns.

A central aspect of my discussion is that, as far as its being a film about youth, *The Social Network* is a threshold case, in terms of the age of its protagonists, as well as of its broader production and exhibition contexts. Fincher and Sorkin's film raises questions about who this film is actually *for*, but by the same token, what it is we expect movies about or for 'youth' to actually do, or represent. In terms of this book, then, and its situation within the wider series, one needs to consider a key question: How might one define 'youth cinema', and where does *The Social Network* sit within such frameworks?

An issue one needs to engage with is that ideas and discussions around 'youth cultures' on screen tend to focus more frequently on teenagers, as opposed to the college-age cast of characters in *The Social Network*. The specificity of this particular demographic, both as the subject and audience of a genre, is highlighted by the use of the word 'teen', 'teenager', or 'adolescence' in many of the now-canonical studies of youth film (Considine 1985; Lewis 1992; Doherty 2002; Shary 2005; Driscoll 2011). On the other hand, Timothy Shary's *Generation Multiplex: The Image of Youth in Contemporary American Cinema* (2002), and his co-edited volume with Alexandra Seibel, *Youth Culture in Global Cinema* (2007), which include films with older pro-tagonists, both challenge the limitations of looking at youth culture in film predominantly through the frame of (American) high schools and their associated spaces. The Cinema and Youth Cultures series, in which this present book appears, has in fact done the same. While it has paid due attention to some of the widely recognised US teen films (*Grease* (Kleiser 1978), *The Breakfast Club* (Hughes 1985), *Clueless* (Heckerling 1995), *Easy A* (Gluck 2010)), as well as recent revisions of the teen-film paradigm (*The Hunger Games* (Ross 2012), *Boyhood* (Linklater 2014), *Moonlight* (Jenkins 2016)), it has also identified the significance of 'youth cultures' beyond teenage itself: whether in the prolonged adolescent cultures at work in *Clerks* (Smith 1994), *Big Wednesday* (Milius 1978) or *A Hard Day's Night* (Lester 1964), or the European Erasmus-scheme collectives in *L'Auberge Espangole* (Klapisch 2002). As I will argue, inasmuch as *The Social Network* establishes a particular territory around its enclaves of Harvard and Palo Alto, the film fits neatly within these broader terms of youth film; in this instance, extending aspects of youth's irresponsibility, rebelliousness and freedoms to the terrains of college life and Silicon Valley innovation.

Narrative representation, of course, in terms of the ages of char-acters and particular social settings, is not the only marker through which one might assess youth film. The position the film takes with regard to these characters, and how an audience might feel about them, also matters. As Shary has argued, the particular appeal and academic interest of (in this case) teen films is that they 'spoke to us in our adolescence'. Every generation, he continues, 'witnesses its ... ideas and expectations, its fantasies and fears, presented in the images of youthful characters coming of age' (Shary 2005: 3). Shary's point may be quite broad, but he nevertheless highlights the way films about youth are to a large extent defined by the relationship young people have to them, and the degree to which such films offer some kind of reflection or point of identification for their own youthful audience.

Looking at *The Social Network* from this perspective raises some issues. As I will discuss, Fincher and Sorkin's film is notable for its absence of grown-ups, or at least, grown-ups who actually have any meaningful bearing on the action of the film. Yet it remains a film made mostly by adult males, from the generation prior to that of Zuckerberg and company. As Shary has reminded us elsewhere, 'screen images of youth have always been traditionally filtered through adult perspectives', mostly in terms of the adults who make the films (Shary 2002: 3). In the case of *The Social Network*, Sorkin and Fincher were forty-eight and forty-seven when the film went into production. Scott Rudin, one of the film's producers, was fifty-one; while two of its other producers, Michael de Luca and Dana Brunetti, were respectively in their forties and late thirties. *The Social Network* is officially adapted from a book, *The Accidental Billionaires*, by Ben Mezrich, who was forty-one. Even Trent Reznor and Atticus Ross, who co-produced the film's score, were in their forties when they worked on the film.

As Shary's point underlines, these are hardly exceptional contexts for youth film, or for Hollywood film production more generally. On this point, we should also remind ourselves that *The Social Network*, unlike a number of the youth films mentioned earlier, does not emerge out of a US independent scene often associated with a younger generation of filmmakers, writers and producers (King 2009). Fincher and Sorkin's film is, by contrast, a major studio film, produced by Columbia Pictures, and distributed by Sony Pictures Releasing – both part of the Sony Pictures Motion Picture Group. In the same way, then, that it is important on my part to acknowledge my own generational position in terms of viewing this film, one needs to consider the significance of this film being made by a group of – let's face it – other middle-aged (white) men.

Notably, Sorkin himself has acknowledged his own ambivalence towards the very subject he was hired to write about, admitting that he had not signed up to Facebook until he signed on for *The Social Network*. The screenwriter nevertheless adds that he became fascinated by the capacity for personal re-invention generated by the platform: the way that a user, for example, may use their profile and updates effectively to turn themselves into 'Ally McBeal [or] Carrie Bradshaw' (quoted in Grossman 2010). Sorkin notes in the same interview the complex background to the story that attracted him to it: not so much the technology or the broader implications of Facebook itself, but rather 'the story' that its creation offered: one about 'friendship and loyalty, class, jealousy, betrayal' (ibid.). Following accusations around the time of its release that *The Social Network* was sexist – a reasonable claim, which I will address at a later point – Sorkin went on record to defend his screenplay, suggesting, revealingly, that he did not focus on 'women who challenge [the men]' because 'no woman who could challenge them would be interested in being anywhere near them' (Barkhorn 2010). One woman who *has* very publicly challenged male authority and sexism, but also seems comfortable being near Zuckerberg, is Facebook's long-time COO and author of *Lean In*, Sheryl Sandberg. According to Sorkin, at a private screening, Sandberg rebuked the producers of *The Social Network* for what she saw as the film's cruel treatment of her young boss: 'How can you do this to a kid?' she is alleged to have asked (quoted in Sorkin 2019). Sorkin's reply to Sandberg remains unknown, but he *has* acknowledged that, from his perspective, he was writing about 'a very angry and deeply misogynistic group of people' (Barkhorn 2010). The type of empathetic distance implied here from its subjects inevitably raises questions about how a given viewer, and above all a young one, is really supposed to feel about such characters.

The Social Network, with its emphasis on damaged individuals building empires, can in fact be seen more as part of a continuity within Sorkin's television and film work, extending to his recent screenplays for *Steve Jobs* (Boyle 2015), about the Apple founder and former CEO, and *Molly's Game* (Sorkin 2017), about the skier-turned-entrepreneur who ran a string of clandestine, high-stakes poker games in Los Angeles and New York during the 2000s. In their shared emphasis on business, backstabbing and retribution – all three films, at their heart, depict bruised protagonists using entrepreneurial acumen to enact some form of revenge, and exercise power – these films engage with the rapacious, Darwinian contest of innovation and capitalism, featuring protagonists whose drive towards their creative or economic goals is matched only by their lack of interest in sustaining friendships or good reputations.

Sorkin's work on either side of these films – such as his writing for the television series *The West Wing* (Warner Bros. 1999–2006) and, more recently, the courtroom drama *The Trial of the Chicago 7* (Sorkin 2020) – highlights the more utopian elements of his authorship, from the civics lessons and 'liberal vision' highlighted in the former (Frame 2014: 114), to the championing of free speech and right to protest in the more recent film. Yet by their own nature, even *The West Wing* and *The Trial of the Chicago 7* are also fundamentally about *winning*, and about the American political and legal systems as games that can be exploited by the canniest player. In *The Social Network*, similarly, mastery over one's competitors and peers, and the ability to make brutal decisions in the business's interest, are part of the territory in this pursuit of billion-dollar companies. It is one of the serendipities of the Facebook story and *The Social Network* in turn that two of its main characters, the twins Cameron and Tyler (Winklevoss), are elite rowers and aspiring Olympians, since their own drive to finish first provides the dramatic foil to Mark's own ambitions. One of the stories emerging from the film is that perennial 'winners' like Cameron and Tyler do not hold the same advantages within the new digital land-scape, but it is still the hyper-masculine world of sports that persists as an analogy for this emerging economy. 'That's life in NFL', says Justin Timberlake's Sean (Parker), moments after the ejection of Eduardo (Saverin) from the Facebook offices, and in response to Mark's dis-comfort.[2] Sean echoes here an earlier Sorkin line from Season 1 of *The West Wing* when the president's Deputy Chief of Staff compliments Vice President Hoynes on a smart political move made to garner votes for a bill. 'Welcome to the NFL', Hoynes replies, comparing political life to the hardball of US sports' most competitive and injury-strewn franchise; while also, as Sean does here in *The Social Network*, tacitly acknowledging the meritocracy of top players – within which, of course, they by inference include themselves.

How one assesses this fact is in many respects to come to terms with the morality of the twenty-first century's social media-dominated culture. Mark's somewhat uncertain motivations and often dama-ging actions do little throughout the film to dispel the opinion – ex-pressed at the beginning by Erica, the one female character in the film who does challenge Mark, and then leaves – that he is 'an asshole'. A point to which I nevertheless return is to what extent the film really condemns Mark. The film, like much of Sorkin's broader work, en-gages with the hard, often unsympathetic ambition of its protagonists, but this same ambition and drive either underpin or even provide the justification and motivation for the very things he writes about: be-coming, and remaining, President of the USA; turning Apple into the world's biggest company; inventing and building Facebook, the world's largest social media network.

Indeed, Richard Brody (2010), in a *New Yorker* feature on *The Social Network*, astutely draws a parallel between the fervent en-trepreneurial drive of Facebook's creation and the creative energies of Hollywood itself. As a screenwriter and now director working in Hollywood, Sorkin himself will hardly be a stranger to the notion that ambition and competitiveness are necessary qualities for realizing your artistic goals. The executive and creative power both the writer and director of *The Social Network* now wield may blind us to the fact that such power was not given automatically, and that Sorkin's and

Fincher's formative experiences in the business enable them to see parallels between their own careers – at an earlier point in their lives – and those of the Facebook founder.

Fincher, significantly, has stated that he had 'an enormous amount of empathy for Mark Zuckerberg', comparing in this case his own memory of his younger self as a creative innovator dealing with 'a bunch of grownups', and frustrated by their adult miscomprehension (quoted in Grossman 2010). The attractiveness of the Facebook story for Fincher, as he put it, was that it showed 'a bigger truth about the last seven years [2003–10], and a bigger truth about what it is to be youthful and have a dream and enthusiasm' (ibid.). Fincher's own complex relationship to the story reflects the ambivalence that runs throughout the film. As much as we might *know* that the film is depicting some often terrible behaviour, from young men of questionable ethics, *The Social Network* still seeks to carry us relentlessly forward via its protagonists' youthful energy and enthusiasms.

The Social Network is something of a companion film to 2015's *Steve Jobs*, and while the events narrated in the former post-date the latter's by several years, together the two films form a biographical diptych spanning a fertile, ultimately age-defining era of technological innovation and industry. Sorkin's script is based loosely on Walter Isaacson's generous biography of Jobs, though one which also introduces its subject as '[neither] a model boss or human being' (Isaacson 2011: xix). Sorkin's script for *Steve Jobs* is unsparing about the Apple CEO's capacity for cruelty: his initial lack of concern for, and denial of, his biological daughter; his disregard for technical and time limitations in the demands he makes on his employees; his callous treatment of one-time friends and collaborators such as Steve Wozniak, whose role in the film as sympathetic fall guy is not dissimilar to that of Eduardo in *The Social Network*. But both Jobs', and *Steve Jobs*' eventual point is that these things, while they matter, and while they are not socially forgivable, may be in this instance by-products of something artistically indelible: the work, the things that get made, the reason why their story is being told in the first place. As an exchange near the end of the film between 'Woz' and Steve summarizes it:

WOZ: When people used to ask me what the difference was between me and Steve Jobs I'd say Steve was the big picture guy and I liked a solid workbench. When people ask me what the difference is now I just say Steve's an asshole. Your products are better than you are, brother.

STEVE: That's the idea, brother.

'Move fast and break things'. This is not something anyone ever says in *The Social Network*, though as I discuss later, it became Facebook's unofficial motto in its early years, exemplifying the company's desire to do things because they are there to be done – and sometimes, without due consideration of the consequences. Infamy, inevitably, has to jostle with renown in this regard. Having a reputation does not always mean having a *good* reputation, but then, in order to do something, both *Steve Jobs* and *The Social Network* suggest, how can you ensure the latter? Sean underlines this point in a terse exchange with the Facebook president he aims to replace:

SEAN: You think you know me. Right?
EDUARDO: I've read enough.
SEAN: You know how much I've read about you? *Nothing.*

The Social Network is generous to Eduardo, whose ousting from Facebook proceeds from Sean's own encroachment into the company, and the denial of his invaluable economic contribution to the company's birth. One ambiguity of the film, nevertheless, is to entertain the possibility that Sean, for all his slipperiness and pretensions, might be *right*. Just as *Steve Jobs* asks whether, in the historical scheme of things, making beautiful products might be more significant than being a beautiful person, *The Social Network* asks whether creating Facebook might be worth losing your good name – especially, Sean hints, if losing your good name is tantamount to finding one actually worth having.

The 'Adultification' of Youth Film

This may have seemed a roundabout way to broach the question of *The Social Network*'s situation within youth cinema, but there is a very specific point to be made here; namely, the point at which youth, and films about them, encroach on territories previously colonized by an older generation – such as business, the economy, technological innovation, the control and dissemination of information. In this respect, it is also important to see *The Social Network* within evolving industrial and generic contexts for 'youth' film more broadly in the twenty-first century, and above all in Hollywood, where we witness not only a conflation of erstwhile adult and teen genres, but a shift on the part of youth cinema towards the industrial mainstream. Following the intermittent peaks in film production and reception cycles – and in particular, the golden period of the mid-1980s to the late 1990s – the staple genre of the 'teen film', to take this once dominant example, has proved less reliable in box-office terms. Surveying the field around the time of *The Social Network*'s production, Elissa Nelson identifies a decline in the fortunes of this commercial genre. While there is no shortage of such films produced in the USA around this same period – *17 Again* (Steers 2009), *Easy A*, *Chronicle* (Trank 2012) and *The Perks of Being a Wallflower* (Chbosky 2012) being just a few of Nelson's examples – these were mostly 'small-scale, small-budget' films with much lower box-office returns in comparison to golden-era films such as *The Breakfast Club*, *Ferris Bueller's Day Off* (Hughes 1986) or *Clueless*. In fact, across the period Nelson surveys, only three productions identifiable as teen films – *Juno* (Reitman 2007), *Superbad* (Mottola 2007) and *The Fault in Our Stars* (Boone 2014) – broke into the top twenty-five at the North American box office in their respective years (Nelson 2017: 127).

The contexts for such comparative decline, or at least re-scaling of commercial expectations, are varied. One might, for example, point to the competition from delivery systems like Netflix and other digital providers, or a turn on the part of Hollywood's traditionally dominant youth demographic towards videogames and other interactive media (Nelson 2017: 128–9). As Betty Kaklamanidou has argued, films about youth are not so much adapting to successive generations (who are less interested in cinema than previous ones), but sticking and ageing with the same audience that grew up watching teen movies in the 1980s and 1990s (Kaklamanidou 2018: 28). On the one hand, this has encouraged a more self-reflexive and ironic aspect to the genre (in films such as *Easy A*, to use Kaklamanidou's own film of choice); while on the other, there is a turn towards youthful protagonists that are simply *older*, to the point of not being 'young' at all – the case in point here being the 'man-child' comedies of writer-director Judd Apatow, such as *The Forty Year-Old Virgin* (Apatow 2005) and *Knocked Up* (Apatow 2007) (29).

Meanwhile, the more broadly inclusive 'family film' genre, extending from Disney-Pixar films to the *Harry Potter* series (2001–11), has encroached on territory previously colonized by films targeted more exclusively, and classified more restrictively, at teens. Nelson identifies the way erstwhile narrative elements of the teen film – adolescent protagonists, 'coming-of-age stories', a focus on everyday struggles and romance – are now integrated within the industrial demands of a contemporary Hollywood looking to attract broader demographics, and driven by the commercial possibilities of the franchise film (Nelson 2017: 131; see also Brown 2013; Archer 2019). The 'teen' has not exactly gone away, following this argument; but in terms of her visibility in mainstream Hollywood, she is more recently seen in film series, often adapted from existing 'Young Adult' fiction, such as the *Hunger Games* (2012–15), *Twilight* (2008–12), *Divergent* (2014–16) and *Maze Runner* (2014–15) films; or in comic-book adaptations such as the various *Spider-Man* iterations (2002), or the *Kick-Ass* movies (2010, 2013).

Significantly for this present study, Nelson's argument highlights the transformed expectations of youth in twenty-first-century Hollywood cinema, resituated on a broader stage than the often quite intimate or institutional settings of prior teen films. From one point of view, then, the repositioning of youth in *The Social Network* within the field of mainstream, 'adult' production is entirely coherent within the terms Nelson highlights. The closeness in production contexts between *The Social Network* and the earlier *21* (Luketic 2008) offers another instance of this re-positioning of youth towards more 'adult' cinematic fields. Made by some of the same production team as *The Social Network* (Michael de Luca and Dana Brunetti), and also distributed by Sony Pictures, *21* was another adaptation of a book by Mezrich: in this instance, *Bringing Down the House* (2002), about the real-life team of MIT students who, employing card-counting and probability analysis, attempted to make a killing at the Las Vegas blackjack tables. I will return to the links between *21* and *The Social Network* in the next chapter; for now, though, it is worth noting how both films depict 'youth' as a demographic *already* grappling with the professional and material demands, as well as competing for social and economic power, in a way more readily associated with 'adult' cinematic fare.

What, indeed, links Nelson's discussion to both *21* and *The Social Network*, albeit in a somewhat skewed and capitalistic sense, is its focus on the transformed weight of expectation carried by youth in more recent Hollywood cinema. As Nelson concludes, the teen protagonists of franchises like *The Hunger Games* 'are positioned as needing to balance personal growth along with being saviors' (2017: 133). Exactly what Mark and his peers in *The Social Network* might be trying to 'save' is a point for debate, but what the latter film does at least share with its franchise peers is the sense that, within the climate of the early twenty-first century, *it is already too late to be young*. There is no time for 'personal growth' since the world has to be saved – or in the case of *The Social Network*, conquered. Speed, as I discuss in the second chapter of this book, is fundamental to one's understanding of *The Social Network*, and to a large degree many of the films Nelson highlights are also about this *acceleration* of youth, if not the loss of youth itself, within this contemporary environment.

Accompanying this sense of accelerated responsibility is a focus on youth as being more self-sufficient, isolated even from the parental generation. As Kaklamanidou points out, various evolving iterations of youth film in America have focused on parents and the parental generation as structuring components of such films' narratives: from the rejection of parental mores and values in the 1950s through to the late 1960s; to the 'troubled family' films of the late 1970s and early 1980s; to the ever-present but always 'square' parents and authority figures in the John Hughes cycle of teen films, and subsequent teen films made in its wake (Kaklamanidou 2018: 66). What makes *The Social Network* significant in this context is that Mark and his colleagues have no apparent concern with parents, or adults generally: forging any understanding or alliance with the older generation is not these protagonists' concern. The only grown-ups we see in the film are lawyers, in the film's various deposition scenes, or often derided figures of authority: the Harvard IT supervisor and the disciplinary panel, made to seem technologically obsolete by the Facemash episode; a condescending computer science lecturer, humbled by Mark's dismissive answer to a notionally testing question; or even, in some respects, Lawrence Summers, the former Treasury Secretary turned Harvard President, who does not seem to understand what all the fuss is about. Whatever Mark's motivations in the film, pleasing or rebelling against parental figures does not seem to be one of them. Mark's only contestation with adult authority, in fact, at one of the litigation sessions, is simply for wasting his time; for keeping him stuck in a room while he could be back at Facebook, doing things, as he arrogantly informs these highly-qualified adults, 'that no one in this room … is intellectually or creatively capable of'.

There is another sense here in which *The Social Network* takes the framework proposed by Nelson, yet twists it with an entrepreneurial inflection. The idea of 'surviv[ing] adolescence' (2017: 128) which in the contexts of, say, *The Breakfast Club* or even *Mean Girls* (Waters 2004), has merely a figurative connotation, assumes within the evolving contexts of series such as *The Hunger Games* or *Divergent* an entirely literal meaning. For Mark Fisher, there is a specific generational politics informing these series' dystopian narratives: he views them as reflecting the anxiety and distrust brought on by anthropogenic climate change and economic precarity. A series such as *The Hunger Games*, he speculates, has 'no doubt resonated so powerfully with its young audience because it has engaged feelings of betrayal and resentment rising in a generation asked to accept that its quality of life will be worse than that of its parents' (Fisher 2012: 27). *The Social*

Network touches on a similar distancing from the parental generation but focuses instead on what we might call the techno-utopian flipside to these contexts: one in which a particular constituency of digitally proficient youth actually get to live lives that are creatively and materially *way beyond* anything their parents could have imagined.

Like many of the lines Sorkin gives Mark in *The Social Network*, the litigation scene put-down quoted above is grounded in his real-life counterpart's biography: the line here echoes Zuckerberg's reported 2007 statement, made during an event at Stanford, that 'young people are just smarter' (quoted in Coker 2007). Mark's/Zuckerberg's comments are rooted in an essentially generational recognition that millennials *can* find their way around computers and other digital technologies – technologies that will shape the coming world, albeit in the image of young people like them – in ways their parents or even their teachers cannot possibly do. Whether or not his generation is necessarily 'smarter', they can do this because they happen to be born into a generation for whom such technologies are 'native', and their everyday interactions and educations revolve around them.[3] At the same time, though, this defining connection to technology, and especially the Internet, is what separates *this* particular generation of young people not just from its parents, but from other, earlier iterations of youth culture and the films made about them. This same generation – specifically, the ones attending elite colleges during the era in which *The Social Network* is set – is arguably one of the most well-educated and well-provided for generations in history, as well as being the most technologically well-connected (Kaklamanidou 2018: 61). It is one of the consequent ironies of *The Social Network*, then, that its protagonists' seeming disregard for parental figures or grown-ups in general, and their somewhat forced rebellious pose, is a corollary of their materially comfortable and supportive family backgrounds – a point to which I will return in Chapter 3.

'This Is Off the Record': The Serious Fiction of *The Social Network*

As I discuss in the final chapter of this book, some commentators have criticized *The Social Network* for either softening or exaggerating its real-life points of reference; and in approaching *The Social Network* generally, it is important to bear in mind that the film remains a *fictional* treatment of its subject matter. Certain scenes and sections of dialogue are drawn from first-person recollection, legal transcripts from the depositions dramatized in the film, and more reliably (as actual evidence), from existing blog posts and emails written by Zuckerberg at the time. How much one might understand *The Social Network* as a 'document' of its young protagonists and the founding of Facebook, though, is questionable. One complication is Mezrich's *The Accidental Billionaires*, on which Sorkin's screenplay is officially based (though more accurately, the film is based on Mezrich's book proposal: Sorkin wrote the screenplay concurrently with Mezrich's own project (Harris 2010)). Mezrich, a former science fiction and *X-Files* writer, has himself acknowledged that his technique blurs the lines between fictional and factual writing, admitting that he is 'not a journalist', but rather someone 'attempting to tell a really cool story' and 'essentially handling Hollywood these ready-made movies ... in the form of books' (quoted in Karim 2020).

The nature of this approach inevitably raises questions around *The Accidental Billionaires*' claim to historical record. Mezrich's signature style is to recount 'true' stories in a novelistic fashion, using interior monologue, free-indirect discourse and punchy dialogue, anchored to a specific timeline of events. For all his books' popularity (and possibly for this same reason), their detractors see them as problematic, sensationalist embellishments of truth, based in hearsay and speculation, with a casual attitude to contextual accuracy (Maslin 2009; Harris 2009). Elliot Schrage, Facebook's head of communications when *The Accidental Billionaires* was published, and in a move designed to downplay the book's qualities as reportage, even suggested that Mezrich 'clearly aspires to be the Jackie Collins or Danielle Steele of Silicon Valley' (quoted in Harris 2009).

Arguably, though, the excesses and more melodramatic aspects of *The Accidental Billionaires*, and indeed the film it inspired, might prove its most revealing characteristics. The more sensational elements of Mezrich's book may give the reader pause; just as the shenanigans and back-stabbings dramatized in the eventual film might, among some viewers, be viewed with a slight pinch of salt. In some respects, though, the book and film actually *under*play the viciousness of which Zuckerberg, in reality, seems to have been capable, if only in the more unguarded yet indelible spaces of the AOL Instant Messenger (AIM) programme. Unavailable to both Mezrich and Sorkin at the time of writing were the Facebook CEO's AIM exchanges dug up later by *Business Insider*. Here, Zuckerberg makes it quite clear what his intentions were with regard to the Winklevoss team: 'I'm going to fuck them. Probably in the [e]ar'. Later, he boasts about having created a fake 'Cameron Winklevoss' profile on the latter's ConnectU site (the one that started off as Harvard Connection), listing his favourite music as 'the sound of myself masturbating', and his interests as 'trying to find my penis' (quoted in Carlson 2012). But perhaps most striking is Zuckerberg's assessment of Eduardo Saverin and his de facto ejection from the company he helped to found:

> I maintain that he fucked himself ... by completing none of his three assigned tasks ... He failed at all three and he took the offensive against me with no leverage. That just means he's dumb. And now I'm not going to go back to Harvard I don't need to worry about getting beaten by Brazilian thugs. (Ibid.)

In this case, real life seems to offer an even more lurid side of the tale than that provided by the finished fiction.

Whatever its depiction of the truth, the key factor to note here, in terms of *The Social Network*'s status as a youth film, is how and why it got made. This is because the production of the film is in some ways *itself* an act of revenge on the part of the story's ultimate victim. *The Accidental Billionaires* came into being when Saverin, at that time embroiled in the lawsuit we see in the eventual film, wrote to Mezrich explaining that he was the little-known co-founder of Facebook. This untold side of the story in turn became the subject of Mezrich's book and Sorkin's screenplay. As Mezrich acknowledges in his preface, 'Mark Zuckerberg ... declined to speak with me for this book despite numerous requests'; yet the author expresses his gratitude at being 'introduc[ed] to Eduardo Saverin, without whom this story could not have been written' (Mezrich 2009: 2). As sympathetically depicted as Saverin is in both book and film, these depictions tend to mask the wider contexts of the story, in which Saverin, with the help of a hefty settlement, became himself one of the world's richest young men – his fortune (revealed, coincidentally, the same week as Zuckerberg's embarrassing AIM exchanges were unearthed) estimated at nearly $3 billion, over 2 billion of which were represented by his Facebook shares (Solomon 2012). Getting to tell his story in a major Hollywood movie, compensating for his erasure in the wider Facebook narrative, is for Saverin merely the cherry on the top.

What to make of this? Notably, two of the major works on Facebook's history – David Kirkpatrick's *The Facebook Effect* (2010a) and Steven Levy's *Facebook: The Inside Story* (2020) – do not dwell to any extent on the circumstances behind Saverin's departure from Facebook, or its supposed economic and ethical injustices. As Levy pithily notes, after mentioning his successful litigation suit in 2007,

Saverin 'is now known less for what he did or did not do for Facebook than for being the real-life character portrayed by a movie star in *The Social Network*' (2020: 99). Rather than allow this to undermine the significance of Fincher and Sorkin's film, however, I suggest that these circumstances informing the production of *The Social Network* are as equally significant as anything the film purports to represent, given that the film itself exists *as a consequence of* what passed among this particular group of young men, at this particular time in American history. The very nature of these dramatic contexts – the bitchiness, the betrayals, the 'ear-fucking' – play out at once as petulant, vindictive and inevitably *immature* actions, on the part of men whose technological and financial acumen seems matched only by their apparent lack of empathy or humility. The film itself, resulting from Saverin's own bid to make his story heard, is part of this same world, and a part of this same evolving Facebook narrative, rather than a story standing remotely from it.

The epigraph with which I began this Introduction is not, as it happens, about Facebook. Alcorn (the Atari engineer who designed *Pong*) is actually talking about Apple, another company founded by an irreverent 'kid' – Steve Jobs, during his barefoot, non-washing phase – that nevertheless played a key role in transforming the culture of Silicon Valley. Alcorn's jokey observation contains a serious point, though, about the nature of technological entrepreneurship in modern American life: namely, that it is not a respecter of normal rules, and does not need to wait for its innovators to come of age, whatever the messy and disruptive consequences this might entail. Indeed, as I comment at various points in this book, Silicon Valley innovation *tends to* feed off the energies of a younger generation. For good or ill, it is a young person's – typically, a young *man's* – game, one in which 'progress' often goes hand-in-hand with immaturity.

The Social Network is a film born out of these same contexts. In other circumstances, this might make it a film of lesser significance. But it is ultimately the fact that the 'men' in Fincher and Sorkin's film are in reality *boys*, still barely out of high school, and that the tokens over which they fight are not only worth billions of dollars but will shape culture, communication and politics in the ensuing decades, that makes *The Social Network* an important case study within the Cinema and Youth Cultures series. When the financial and reputational stakes are this high, this early in life, something is seriously going on: Fincher and Sorkin's film is testimony to this hitherto unprecedented moment in the lives and history of twenty-first-century youth.

The Chapters

It is a bit more than this, however. As I argue, and as I have already touched upon in this Introduction, as well as being an important cinematic artefact of the current century's culture of 'disruption', *The Social Network* is a significant, and indeed *transitional* text in terms of how one makes sense of a cinema about youth in the twenty-first century. It is not so much that the film 'represents' this disrupted period in our history, but that the film is *itself* 'disruptive', in terms of its relationship to genre, its particular use of mainstream film aesthetics and its depiction of a rebellious yet highly commercialized 'cool'. These central arguments inform the chapters of this book.

In the first chapter, I situate *The Social Network* within the historical contexts of other films about young people and their high school- or college education: probably the most familiar setting, as I note, for youth-oriented films. *The Social Network*, I argue, shows both a continuity with and a departure from this history; above all, in the ways its depictions are in dialogue with earlier films, and at the same time, revise some of the more familiar expectations of how college life is perceived and depicted within this cinematic field. The film, especially, requires a re-engagement with the archetypical figure of the 'geek' in such films, within an era of Silicon Valley-led disruption; an era in which traditional ideas of education and its values are being called into question, precisely by the new technologies and platforms of which Facebook is a dominant example. As I show, *The Social Network* also intersects with wider social and cultural contexts of transforming expectations for young people, and especially students, within this same time. What is education really *for* at this point in our history? This is a question implicitly raised by Fincher and Sorkin's film, with potentially unsettling conclusions (at least for university lecturers like me).

The second chapter considers the aesthetics of *The Social Network*, with a specific focus on speed and 'hacking' as key elements of the film's disruptive stylistic system. As I argue here, *The Social Network* intervenes in a specific period of film history and theory in which an 'accelerated' culture and its attendant cultural forms have become the subject of aesthetic, philosophical and even political debate. If speed (in terms, say, of ever-increasing editing rates) has been problematized in discussions of recent cinema, viewed as symptomatic either of a distracted or unreflective consumerism, this chapter retrieves speed as the very subject and substance of *The Social Network*, linked here to the instantaneous and invasive technologies that would eventually deliver Facebook. In a similar way to Michelle Schreiber, in her observations on Fincher's work (2016), I make the case for the style of *The Social Network* as a kind of new 'digital realism' for the era of Web 2.0; concluding with some observations as to how *The Social Network*, as a depiction and embodiment of such technologies and their impacts, engages with the narratives and values of older cinema – specifically, in this case, with *Citizen Kane* (1941).

One of the key tensions around which *The Social Network* operates is how to reconcile 'cool' with 'capitalism': in other words, how do you sell something when selling is – supposedly – against everything you stand for? This is the focus of the third chapter, which looks closely at how this conundrum runs through the film's screenplay, while also situating the film within the terms of a commodified dissent prevalent in millennial western consumer culture. Focusing on the character of Sean Parker as a 'connector' figure in *The Social Network*, I also consider the film's emphasis on the significance of 'weak ties', and the role of the Internet in enabling these connections, contributing to the unprecedented growth of Facebook during the time in which the film takes place.

Finally, in the last chapter, I look at some commentaries on the film, particularly in terms of the film's evolving legacy during the ten years after its production. As I discuss, the ailing reputation of Facebook and its CEO during these years has – unfairly or otherwise – cast light on the film's critical reception. I acknowledge the importance of such responses, and the difficulties involved in assessing a film based not only on historical record but also on a company as problematic as Facebook, while at the same time, making a final case for the significance of Fincher and Sorkin's film within the broader cinematic depictions of youth in the twenty-first century.

On this final note, I have purposefully avoided in this book giving too much attention to critical reviews of *The Social Network*. These reviews were, in the main, wildly enthusiastic. If I do not touch on them here, it is partly because they are freely available, hardly needing the work of a film scholar to unearth them (unless my task is to direct you in scholarly fashion to the film's Wikipedia page). The more pertinent point, as I explain in Chapter 4, is that such critical responses in themselves do not necessarily tell us much about *The Social Network* as a youth film. As I have noted in this Introduction, to what extent Fincher and Sorkin's film can really be said to be about 'youth' at all is a point of debate. This book makes the case that it is; but as a result, I have limited my engagement with journalistic criticism mostly to commentators and commentaries that either contest or offer support to these views.

Notes

1 I will refer to *The Social Network* throughout as Fincher and Sorkin's film, in part as a personal riposte to *auteur* criticism's tendency to grant disproportionate credit to the director for a film's meaning and effects. In the case of Sorkin, though (a multiple award winner for his earlier work on *The West Wing* (Warner Bros. 1999–2006)), there is already a substantial weight given to Sorkin's authorship of what, as early as 2008, was being described as 'The Aaron Sorkin Facebook Movie' (Kois 2008). Sorkin's credit, notably, is given equal weighting to Fincher's on the packaging of my DVD of the film, further supporting a broader sense of the film's dual authorship in the distribution and promotion of the film.

2 Throughout this book, to avoid confusion, and in keeping with the formatting of Sorkin's screenplay, I refer to the film characters by their first names only. When referring to real-life contexts, I have used either the surname or full name.

3 Steven Johnson (2005: 139–99) has nevertheless made a persuasive case for the increasing intellectual capacity of younger people *as a corollary of* their engagement with digital culture.

1 From Harvard to Palo Alto: The Values of Education in Youth Cinema and *The Social Network*

In a now seminal chapter from his book *Outliers*, Malcolm Gladwell looks at the first major wave of computing entrepreneurs and software designers who formed and shaped the industry in the final decades of the twentieth century: among others, Microsoft's Bill Gates, Paul Allen and Steve Ballmer, Apple founder Steve Jobs and Google CEO Eric Schmidt. What did these men have in common? Ambition? *Genius*? The more prosaic answer, Gladwell argues, is that they all share similar birthdays, each of them being born within a couple of years of each other, or in the case of Gates, Jobs and Schmidt, within just eight months (2008: 35–68). All reached adolescence at a time when computers, a relatively nascent technology, were still the domain of hobbyists or existed as non-portable colossi for which you had to buy and share programming time. If you grew up during this narrow window, however, and just as importantly, had access to computers – as Gates did, thanks to the nearby University of Washington computer centre, or as Jobs did, since he lived near Silicon Valley and got a summer job at Hewlett Packard – then your opportunities increased exponentially.

Gladwell's point is that innovation happens not in isolation, but in the contexts of specific cultural and above all *generational* shifts. In this chapter, similarly, I argue that *The Social Network*, despite its biographical trappings, is not a film simply about one young man. It is more specifically about a *culture*, of which Mark Zuckerberg, albeit one of its most prominent figures, is still just a part. One might discuss this more generally in terms of what has been called 'geek' culture, itself already an important aspect of youth cinema in the twentieth- and current centuries. As I suggest here, though, the use of this somewhat problematic term to describe a type of cultural grouping understates the geek's broader significance and impact. A key point in this chapter is that one makes sense of the 'geek' not as some niche

DOI: 10.4324/9781003161936-2

cultural type, to be called upon only in the particular contexts of youth film. One needs to make sense of this figure in relation to evolving contexts of technology and economics, and above all, to systems and structures of power in both America and the wider global society.

As I have acknowledged here, *The Social Network* inevitably harks back to previous films about youth, and especially those that introduce the geek as either a supporting or (less frequently) central character. As such, one should be encouraged to view Fincher and Sorkin's film as part of a continuity within this cinematic line. In making connections to earlier films, though, there is more than just a film-historical interest in play. Looking at changing representations of the geek historically across cinematic contexts is itself a means of gauging the transformed cultural role of this figure – above all, as one associated with emergent computer technologies and their impacts – in the wider society. A significant aspect of *The Social Network* is in turn the way, within the film's narrative contexts of Web 2.0, that the geek is assuming a more dominant rather than peripheral role; one that in many ways questions and challenges the hierarchical cultural structures that would otherwise, and hitherto, keep them within an allotted place and role, with limited agency.

As *The Social Network* also reminds its viewers, computers, their uses and their related technologies should also be seen in terms of particular *trends*, shaped specifically by the interests of the young, who are typically the earliest technological adopters and most active users. Set in the early 2000s, *The Social Network* depicts a world in which the computer itself has lost some of its prior fascination or exclusivity. This is not because it is no longer relevant, but rather the opposite: the computer is now ubiquitous, banally inserted into the fabric of many viewers', and certainly these characters', everyday lives. Early on in the film, once Mark returns from his break-up with Erica to the haven of his Kirkland rooms, the first thing the film shows is him turn on his two computers. This does not quite describe it, though: Mark's hand actually moves across the devices, the camera shooting the action from the height level of the computers in a medium close-up (Figure 1.1). To use a grammatical analogy, while this might be described as 'Mark turning on the computer', what is actually shown is *the computer being turned on* – or more realistically, the computer being awoken from its temporary sleep in standby mode. What is more, the first words Mark subsequently 'says' in this scene – 'Erica Albright is a bitch' – are actually *written*, in the blog post he ends up writing simultaneously to his creation of Facemash. Note too that when Eduardo arrives not

Figure 1.1 The computer as subject.

long afterwards, the first thing he does is to ask if Mark is okay since he has already heard about his friend's break-up – *on his blog*.

None of this seems especially noteworthy within the contexts of the film's action, but this is precisely the point. As Aaron Tucker has noted in his history of the Internet on film, movies have a tendency to reflect the particular circumstances, anxieties and expectations about new technologies; adding that films made in the wake of the Internet's mainstream emergence during the 1990s – *Hackers* (Softley 1995), *The Net* (Winkler 1995) and even *The Matrix* (Wachowski and Wachowski 1999) – tended to make the Internet a sometimes hyperbolic central dramatic focus. By contrast, the banalization of the Internet in later films, and its repositioning within the background to such stories, suggests the increasing normalization of such technologies (Tucker 2014: 3–4). The casualness with which the computer and its modes of communication are introduced in *The Social Network*, combined with the way they are also placed centrally within the mise-en-scène and dialogue, underscores the point that the film is depicting a cultural and generational tendency rather than an exception. As Steven Levy points out, Zuckerberg's generation, or at least those of sufficient economic privilege and mobility, all came through high school with 'computers attached by modems and ... higher-bandwidth internet. And they had AIM' (2020: 28). The availability of AOL's Instant Messenger, in fact, as already touched upon in the Introduction, shaped the working habits both of Facebook's founder and many of the young men and women who ended up working with him, who often communicated with each other via the service. They were, suggests Levy, '80s kids who had spent the last years of the twentieth century submersed in the chat bubbles on their screens' (2020: 29).

One impact of living one's life through the medium of instant messaging and online publishing is made visible in the same opening scenes, in which Mark's blog post reaches an unsuspecting Erica in her own dorm – though not before it has reached the attention of her male neighbours, who taunt her in the same vein as Mark does. As Erica later reminds Mark, the Internet is written 'in ink' – as Zuckerberg himself, leaving an AIM breadcrumb-trail of his younger self's indiscrete thoughts, would come to realize when things he once messaged came back to 'haunt' him (Levy 2020: 57). Yet it is also this instantaneous connectivity and communication across distance that underpinned the emergence, at the turn of the millennium, of social networking tools. For Zuckerberg, significantly, these tools also enabled the identification and expression of particular personal collective identities, distinct from the prevailing norms of American childhood and adolescence. 'I'm not into baseball, I'm into computers', he would say in a 2010 interview, discussing how much he disliked playing Little League as a boy. For Levy, Zuckerberg's 'begrudging participation on the ballfield [w]as an illustration of something that [Facebook] might one day mitigate': social networks would enable people 'to find their tribes, as opposed to having to endure right field because it was the default activity' (2020: 27).

Zuckerberg's assertion here, made the same year as *The Social Network* was released, offers a segue into the film, which hints at the ways these 'default' American cultures were still largely reiterated and perpetuated by elite institutions such as Harvard University, and more specifically, by the older and (once) dominant cliques within them. Sorkin's screenplay cannily uses its opening dialogue to set up the spectre of Mark's adversaries, Cameron and Tyler, precisely in this vein, via Erica's comments about liking the idea of boys that 'row crew', 'the way a girl likes cowboys'. In narrative terms, the dialogue establishes an element of sexual jealousy and inferiority on the part of Mark (his response to Erica is that guys who row crew 'are bigger than me'): responses that may underpin his subsequent actions. This is probably more Sorkin's writing choice than an actual reflection of the truth, and one could, I believe, happily disregard the insinuation that Facebook was invented as an act of sexually motivated revenge. Yet *The Social Network*'s broader observation is the degree to which certain inherited ideas around the elite cultures of Harvard are bundled up with hierarchies and tensions linked, essentially, to masculine conceptions of power, physicality and prowess. The young men who row crew are not just an arbitrary or casual target of Mark's social and sexual anxieties, since those that *do* row crew – exemplified in the film by Cameron and Tyler – seem also to come from those kinds of backgrounds (WASP, and in this case, from a family 'of means') that form the standard model for entry to the same Final Clubs Mark evidently fails to impress.

Mark's eventual decision to leave Harvard and run Facebook from the West Coast is barely acknowledged in the film, in much the same way that it barely warranted any discussion in real life.[1] An intriguing question in turn is why Mark Zuckerberg went to Harvard *at all*, since his background and interests would perhaps most comfortably lend themselves to more entrepreneurially- and technologically minded colleges like MIT or Stanford, instead of what some view as Harvard's more restrictive academic environment (Levy 2020: 37, 50). That he did not attend the former is fortuitous for *The Social Network*, though, precisely because it provides a more loaded terrain for the kinds of cultural conflicts and transformations the film in part narrates. In one respect, this involves the growing centrality of Palo Alto and Silicon Valley more broadly to the world's economy and balance of power. Stanford University, with its situation near the Bay Area, is a more apt setting for a story about world-altering Internet start-ups, a point which possibly explains why Sorkin, in one of his authorial embellishments, has Sean discovering Facebook in a dorm room there.

But what is more, the screenplay also highlights the point that Sean not only did not go to Stanford but also has not attended college at all ('You're kidding?' replies the girl in whose room he wakes up, as if this possibility is so radical). Indeed, one of the key questions raised by *The Social Network* is not so much the value or significance of particular universities or educational philosophies, but the meaning of university education in the first place. This is not a point made glibly, relying on the exceptional nature of Zuckerberg – like Gates and Jobs before him, two more college drop-out billionaires – to somehow prove a general rule. Rather, the film touches on the value, and even the empirical *substance*, of what one understands university life to offer, and a university degree to provide.

As I will now examine, with reference to some of its cinematic precedents and the discussions around them, *The Social Network* both revisits and rethinks some of the educational archetypes that have shaped many youth films in the preceding years. Its key intervention within this history, I argue, is to situate the emergent figure of the geek – the geek, more specifically, as exemplar of a new technocratic elite – within nuanced, often entangled contexts of class and also ethnic conflict, and of the pursuit of economic or sexual power. To some extent, in looking at the film within the broader history of youth cinema, part of the significance of *The Social Network* is to question and reconfigure largely cinematic conceptions of geek culture vis-à-vis its notional nemesis, in the form of the 'jock': those same kind of guys that 'row crew'. In the process, though, the film also seeks to blur some of the lines hitherto dividing these two cinematic figures. The manner of getting there may differ, but as the film suggests, the intended outcome – mastery of one's social environment, and the attainment of power, through whatever means are available – remains the same.

Seriously Stupid: The Perks of Being an Asshole

Many of the earlier, diverse precedents of *The Social Network* – films, I suggest here, such as *Animal House* (Landis 1978), *Risky Business* (Brickman 1984) *Ferris Bueller's Day Off* and *21* – all highlight the ambivalences of films about youth. One could argue that the youth film is characterized, even defined, by its efforts to take both youth, and the assumed youthful audience, seriously. Yet this effort is often matched only by its serious commitment to representing *immaturity* as youth's defining feature – Catherine Driscoll going so far to suggest that the latter is something such films 'relish' (2011: 76). At the same time, the emerging cultural prominence of the youth film during the 1980s owed much to the ways films like *The Breakfast Club*, *St Elmo's Fire* (Schumacher 1985) or *Some Kind of Wonderful* (Deutch 1987) showed 'a greater depth of understanding' with respect to their teen- or early twenty-something protagonists than had previously been the case (Shary 2005: 68). In truth, though, relishing immaturity while showing depths of understanding is hardly such a contradiction, since a key aspect of this understanding lies in identifying the relevance of education for these same protagonists – or more specifically, its *ir*relevance. Immaturity in these films, at least in relation to schooling, *is* serious business.

Many of the above films demonstrate an irreverence towards both high school and college education. When, early in the film, the title character of *Ferris Bueller's Day Off* tells his parents he wants 'to go to a good college so [he] can have a fruitful life', the banality of the phrase tells us what he *really* thinks: indeed, Ferris's lack of sincerity is only heightened here by our knowledge that he is also lying to his parents in order to play truant. *Ferris Bueller's Day Off*, of course, gives viewers ample reason to align themselves with Ferris and his views: high school is here depicted as a site of tedium, apathy and authoritarianism, the latter embodied by Ferris's nemesis, Principal Rooney. But the somewhat cartoonish depictions at work in the film point to a more striking underlying point about the nature of Ferris's education and his relation to it. Notably, as part of the introduction to Ferris and his world, the film cross-cuts between shots of MTV at Ferris's home and those of his teacher at school, his monotonous voice sending the student body into various states of catatonia. It is not so much school as an institution that is Ferris's problem (he is, as the film later notes, the most popular boy there): it is more the kinds of political and economic history Ferris's classmates are obliged to sit through that mean nothing whatsoever to their present or future concerns. As Ferris (Matthew Broderick) states:

> I do have a test today ... on European socialism. I mean, really, what's the point? I'm not European. I don't plan on being European. So, who gives a crap if they're socialists? They could be fascist anarchists. It still doesn't change the fact that I don't own a car.

Like *Ferris Bueller's Day Off, Risky Business*, made two years previously, takes place at high school, but the film's narrative centres around the significance of getting into the right college (Princeton, in this case), and more specifically, the *financial* benefits of such an education. The early scene in which Joel and his friends discuss their life goals, with almost all of them affirming that they want to 'make lots of money', seems to draw a bleak line over the possibility of a radical student politics or any alternative trajectory in the Reaganite 1980s. Joel (Tom Cruise), who is taking part in a young innovator project at his high school, shows himself in some ways to be an ideal figure for 1980s entrepreneurialism, when he converts his home for one night, in his parents' absence, into a pop-up brothel. When the Princeton admissions officer turns up in the middle of Joel's venture, he ends up staying for the night, literally and figuratively buying into Joel's capitalist venture. Joel subsequently gets the letter of acceptance to Princeton: 'You must have really impressed him', his proud father suggests. The joke, if this is how viewers are invited to read it, is sealed by this final irony: an Ivy League education, in this film's view, both rewards and promotes entrepreneurialism and financial mobility, but the morality of how such mobility is achieved is not a concern. Indeed, in this film, the entrepreneurial drive is encouraged to keep pace with man's – though not necessarily woman's – oldest and most carnal instincts.

In *The Social Network*, Cameron and Tyler, brandishing their Porcellian Club and crew-member status and privileges, nominally represent the sort of Ivy League collegiate ideals that Mark, by comparison, is seen to disregard – or even, with his Facemash project, to bring into disrepute. The twins even seek to charge Mark with breaking the rules of Harvard's gentlemanly 'Standards of Conduct', engineering a meeting with the then Harvard President, Lawrence Summers.[2] Summers, after having dismissed the twins' claims as a purely private matter, makes the point that the innovative spirit of Harvard is not to go into the same old jobs, but to create new ones. Joel's creative salesmanship in *Risky Business* would in effect fit Summers' bill. But so too, Sorkin's script hints, would the twins' plans, had Summers had the clairvoyance to recognize what was really at stake (as Summers says, responding to Cameron and Tyler's suggestion that Harvard Connection is potentially worth millions, 'You might be letting your imaginations run away with you'). Of course, their superficially chivalric morality and pretensions aside, Cameron and Tyler's real-life project was itself little more than an Ivy League-stamped, version 2.0 of Joel's house party in *Risky Business*: a 'dating and socializing site … that would tell [its users] about parties' (Kirkpatrick 2010a: 26). It would also, in words Cameron Winklevoss intended to use on the site, provide 'a list of the hottest clubs and lounges in the Boston area', offering to its users 'reduced admission' (81).

As this example illustrates, a youth-cinema trope that *The Social Network* extends is the disconnect between academic ideals and the actual outcomes of student activities and initiatives. But it also touches on the financial contexts and opportunities, revolving around academic institutions, towards which these films' protagonists also aspire. In the process, the value, both economic and developmental, of these same aspirational institutions is called into question. *21*, as noted in the Introduction, and also based on real events, is the closest precursor film to *The Social Network*. Like the later film, it also takes place in Cambridge, though in this instance at MIT, where we find Ben (Jim Sturgess), a mathematics major, competing for the prestigious and lucrative Robinson Scholarship at Harvard Medical School. *21* dwells mainly on the illicit excitement of the blackjack scheme, perpetrated by a group of MIT's most talented mathematicians and their older instructor, created with the aim of 'bringing down' Las Vegas casinos and reaping the financial rewards in the process. Yet the underlying irony at the heart of *21* is that it only tells this story against the contexts of punitively exclusive tuition fees: Ben is applying for the

Robinson Scholarship because he cannot afford the $300,000 his planned education at Harvard Med is estimated to cost him.

Ben's eventual take up with the blackjack programme, then, is actually premised on economic expediency, not the appeal of a semi-criminal lifestyle. The idea that one might turn to card-counting in Las Vegas to fund a Harvard medical degree of course contains its own satirical value, though like any good satire it has its basis in facts. In *The Social Network*, similar sums of money provide the access to different levels of experience and networking opportunity. The Final Clubs in *The Social Network* recognize Old Money, or at least the ability to make lots of New Money, as a starting point for entrance: as Mark mentions in the opening scene, $300,000, the same figure Ben needs for his tuition in *21*, is also coincidentally the same amount Eduardo has made on stock speculation the summer before the events of *The Social Network* take place. As stated in Mezrich's book, and hinted at in Sorkin's script, this $300,000 is also Eduardo's bargaining chip for entry into the Phoenix Club. In the same way, *21* infers this connection between the possession of capital and the right to educational advancement, networking opportunities, *and* a wild time, *especially* in the most elite academic institutions. From this perspective, Ben's decision to join a clandestine gambling ring to pay for his education is actually drained of its satirical character, in the sense that he is simply levelling an already unfair financial playing field in order to access a desired education.

As the critic Mark Fisher has described it, early twenty-first-century life and culture have been characterized by what he calls 'capitalist realism'; his personal view that the capitalist imagination 'seamlessly occupies the horizon of the thinkable' (2009: 8). Fisher's most telling suggestion with respect to this present book is that, for most teenagers growing up in the West, after the demise both of the Soviet Union and socialist politics, 'the lack of alternatives to capitalism is no longer even an issue' (ibid.), so much have neoliberal economics permeated our everyday interactions and expectations. Fisher's work focuses mainly on the UK, but in a way no less applicable to the US education system. Anya Kamenetz (2006), writing around the time of Facebook's emergence, has described the US college-graduate demographic as a 'generation debt', with students taking on large five-figure loans before entering a highly competitive and increasingly precarious labour market.

In distinction then to the idea of college as an idealized transitional period between childhood and adult responsibility, focused on the

supposedly disinterested virtues of study, university life within neoliberal circumstances becomes increasingly instrumentalized. For one
thing, many students both in the USA and the UK tend to balance
their sizeable debt with jobs in the low-paid 'McDonaldised labour
force', which impinges on their time either for study or socialization in
the very institutions they are paying to attend (McGuigan 2009: 193).
In turn, there is the compulsion, *because* of its expense, and the limited
time in which to engage with studies, simply to scrape through the
exams; all in service of obtaining a qualification which offers only a
modicum of competitive edge in the marketplace. Put together, these
various contexts suggest that, for many students, higher education is at
once expensive, boring, and from an intellectual point of view at least,
entirely pointless (Fisher 2009: 23–6).

As highlighted in the Introduction, the 'accelerated' contexts of
modern youth, in which young people no longer have the time simply
to be young, are hardly lost on twenty-first-century youth cinema. As I
suggested previously, while from a production point of view *The Social
Network* might be a corollary of such wider tendencies in the youth
film, it would be misguided to situate Fincher and Sorkin's film within
these same frameworks. One obvious contrast is that, unlike many of
the beleaguered adolescents of the teen franchise film – living, as Fisher
describes it elsewhere, in a precarious world 'stripped of (job and social) security … trapped in a perpetual present tense, unable to plan or
dream' (2012: 33) – Mark and his peers are very much on the other side
of this equation. There is no sense at all in the film that any of the
latter are going to 'fail' in the commonest sense of the term. Even in
the first scene, Erica tacitly complements Mark by suggesting he will
likely become 'a very successful computer person': something of an
understatement in the course of things. None of the film's litigants,
meanwhile, Eduardo included (as the end sequence reminds us), are
likely to be claiming unemployment benefits any time soon. Indeed,
the fact that the film can potentially generate sympathy for Eduardo,
whose remuneration, even with its dilution, is still likely to be in seven-
figure sums, is telling, so steeped is it in a world where – as Sean reminds Mark and Eduardo – prestige, success and 'cool' are no longer
measured in millions of dollars, but in *billions*. The distinction is that,
in terms of the youth film, whereas this success might normally be
achieved through the pursuit of valued college degrees, characters like
Mark are now rejecting such paths. All of which raises the question:
What in the world of *The Social Network* is an elite college like
Harvard actually *for*?

Figure 1.2 Creative irresponsibility in Palo Alto.

Animal House Revisited

That Facebook is to some extent a by-product and outcome of Mark and his friends' most hedonistic antics is a particular view the film does not shirk. The drunken atmosphere surrounding the intern interviews, for instance, or the 'bro-grammer' vibe surrounding the nascent company's Palo Alto residence, with its pool, zip-wires and bongs, encourage a view of Facebook as emerging from the same atmosphere of dorm-room pranks that brought Facemash to light (Figure 1.2). This emphasis on irresponsibility is hardly a new feature of the youth film, as noted earlier, and films about college, perhaps even more than those about high school, have embraced this idea.

As a transitional space suspended between the end of childhood and the beginning of adult responsibility, colleges, both in reality and as depicted in cinema, effectively enable the temporary carnival of sex, drugs and partying that defers entry into grown-up life (Driscoll 2011: 79).[3] While a very different film from *Risky Business*, *National Lampoon's Animal House* (1978), set at the fictional Faber University, is no less satirical with regard to educational institutions. *Animal House* was filmed at a time, shortly after Vietnam and Watergate, when the integrity of the US government was being called into question. Delta House (the 'animal house' in question), with its hard-drinking, anarchic and academically under-achieving members, is in the scheme of the film a test case for an American system that notionally claims to stand for individual liberties, but which would still make the ultra-conservative, militaristic Omega House, Delta's nemesis, the only real training ground for 'future social leaders' (Driscoll 2011: 78). Driscoll's point is that, in the inverted spirit of carnival, the whole American system in *Animal House* is turned on its head. And yet, the film's more striking relevance to this present study lies in the fact that some of the more excessive aspects of its satire get played out, only this time for 'real', in *The Social Network*.

John Landis's cult film has become something of a byword for collegiate-style debauchery: indeed, Mezrich, in his self-consciously cinematic way, writes of the Alpha Epsilon Pi party – the Jewish fraternity 'Caribbean Night', where Mark first suggests to Eduardo his idea for building a social network – that 'it wasn't exactly a scene from *Animal House*' (2009: 13). As with many genre films, *Animal House* offers an ideological cushion against actual circumstances, reveling in its reassurance that the best times at Faber are being had by those students clearly *not* marked for 'future social leader' status. Its implication is that the types welcomed by Omega are too frigidly bound by tradition and obscure social ritual to actually enjoy themselves. While the *really* good time is always happening across campus at Delta, Omega only has time for monastic initiation ceremonies and homoerotic flagellation rituals, led by students who can seemingly only rise to the occasion, as it were, when it involves army-corps drills or the repression of Delta House members.

Superficially, the uber-WASPs Cameron and Tyler may stand in for the equally WASP-ish leaders at Omega, who share the twins' preoccupation with university regulations and codes of conduct. This is a very limited view, though. For one thing, the more radical ploy of *The Social Network* is to draw parallels between Delta's social 'losers' and the dorm-room clique that, with Facebook, actually *did* go on to be 'future social leaders' of sorts, only on a more massive scale. In *Animal House*, intellectual and professional ambition can only be derided. *The Social Network* is different since the film hardly debunks intellectual and creative achievement in itself – Facebook, as Mark reminds his listeners in the deposition scenes, exemplifies such work and the distinctive skills of his employees. What the film *does* do, however, is uncouple such work and achievements from the same institutions, traditions and authority figures that would previously espouse it and nominally underpin its value. As with *21*'s treatment of its blackjack-playing undergrads, *The Social Network* highlights the creative work of the teens that built Facebook, while at the same time, emphasizing Facebook's distance from some of the notional aims and ideals of college education.

The link between Kirkland and Delta houses also runs aground, inasmuch as the hedonistic antics enjoyed by Delta in the latter film are hardly out of reach for Omega's Old-School counterparts in *The Social*

Network. In fact, the broader irony in *The Social Network* is that such debauchery, and sex in particular, structures a significant part of university interaction at a profound level. Mark expresses as much in the film when, quizzed by his room-mate Dustin about a girl in one of his classes, he has the epiphany that sends him running off to complete the site, adding 'Relationship Status' and 'Interested In' to the user page. As he explains to Eduardo: 'This is what drives life at college. Are you having sex or aren't you. It's why people take certain classes, and sit where they sit, and do what they do'. As much as this is seen by Mark as the final part of the motor driving Facebook, Mark also tacitly acknowledges that Facebook will facilitate sexual interaction on campus. More to the point, it will facilitate sexual interaction for those on campus without privileged access to its possibilities; in other words, to students like Dustin, Eduardo and Mark.

The idea that *The Social Network* might ultimately be about little more than sex – about who has the status and power to get it, and what further status and power sex infers – may be one of the film's most profoundly comic but also disturbing aspects. The hierarchical distinctions of social mobility and access in the film – the separations, say, between Mark and his friends, and the Final Clubs from which they are (mostly) excluded – are marked in terms of the mainly heterosexual opportunities such interactions might afford. The Phoenix Club party we see in the film, spliced within Mark's creation of Facemash, may exist largely in Mark's mind, although Erica *has* already alluded to the local girls bussed in from around the Cambridge area so they might 'party with the next Fed chairman'. Colloquially at least, as Mezrich puts it, this bus was known as the 'Fuck Truck': one which 'all socially knowledgeable Harvard grads had been on ... at least once in their college career' (2009: 72). But since this bus only came around occasionally, Cameron and Tyler's plans for Harvard Connection, it seems, were to extend the range and frequency of possible encounters, albeit only for designated users: those benefiting, in this case, from their 'H-Bomb' ('Harvard Male') status (30–1).

This is the final but crucial element that links *The Social Network* to *Animal House*, while also rethinking the latter in more bleakly comic terms. While *Animal House* seeks to amuse with the idea that future leaders are products of their own homo- or heterosexual repression, *The Social Network*, by contrast, suggests the opposite. Sex in this film is another form of capital, with access to it as much socially inherited as acquired. At an overt structural level, the pursuit and acquisition of sex is the dynamic that shapes *The Social Network*, aligning it in turn with a history of youth films preceding it, from *Animal House* to

Porky's (Clark 1981), from *American Pie* (Weitz 1999) to *Superbad*. Inasmuch though as losing one's virginity, or simply getting laid, is not really the narrative destination of Fincher and Sorkin's film – this happens to both Mark and Eduardo by the mid-point – *The Social Network* is very different from those previous films. *The Social Network*, indeed, and like *Risky Business* before it, goes further, in its insinuation that sex has much further-reaching implications than simply being a teenage or collegiate rite-of-passage in the hiatus of school or college life. Sex, rather, is imbricated in the accumulation, the structures and the (ab)uses of power in society more broadly. And more to the point, as *The Social Network* suggests, the 'geeks' are on it too, since it is largely through technology that erstwhile hierarchies of sexual opportunity and acquisition are undermined.

Viewers have already seen within the first ten minutes of *The Social Network* that the film engages with the possibilities for sexual intrusion and violence brought on by the Internet, perpetrated by anyone in possession of both a laptop and sufficient programming skills. Michele Schreiber underlines the points that Mark, even if he might see himself as different from the guys that row crew, is merely 'enacting his own form of technological degradation' of women by creating Facemash: an activity that simply reproduces through technological means what he imagines the young men of the Final Clubs are already doing *in situ* (2016: 13). This more sexually exploitative aspect of the cinematic geek is not entirely alien to the longer history of youth film. As Driscoll argues with regard to 1980s teen films such as *Weird Science* (Hughes 1986), where two boys actually build their fantasy woman, or *Revenge of the Nerds* (Kanew 1984), their protagonists still 'seek recognition of their masculinity through the authority of sexual partners'; Driscoll's conclusion being these films offer mostly 'a new variation on old questions about how one becomes a man' (2011: 49). *The Social Network* offers little revision of these tropes. Indeed, from Zuckerberg's point of view, the Facemash experiment was just an extension of what many students were already doing with existing documents: the hard-copy Freshman Register, for example, which displayed profiles of all entering students, was often 'extensively annotated' by boys who 'would circle photos of the best looking girls' (Kirkpatrick 2010a: 28).

'A Diversity Thing': Jewishness and Social Structure

As my discussion so far suggests, the already tenuous separation of geek and jock that underpins a key part of youth film culture, especially in US film, is blurred still further in *The Social Network* by its depiction of sex, and the pursuit of it by protagonists across this somewhat illusory divide. The problem with discussing Fincher and Sorkin's film with reference to such distinctions is that, in the contexts of its Harvard setting, these binaries tend to collapse under the over-arching weight of educational privilege – added to the fact that, jock or geek, the film is only ever depicting a conflict between different kinds of socially- and economically advantaged white men. Where then, if at all, is the distinction? Is it simply technological prowess within shifting technological terrains that mark the difference between the boys at Alpha Epsilon Pi, and the denizens of Harvard's boathouse?

The specific foregrounding in the film of Harvard's Jewish fraternity offers some matter for discussion here since it emphasizes the different strata of expectation, connection and power wielded within the sometimes overly broad terms of 'white male' hegemony. If the film, its references to Alpha Epsilon Pi aside, is not always explicit in its en-gagement with Jewishness, the *absence* of a more overt discussion of Jewishness might be precisely the point, since the film highlights an ambivalence and tension on Mark's part in terms of how his back-ground impacts upon his bid for Final Club membership. The sight of Eduardo, Dustin and others at the Caribbean Night, huddled in a pack discussing the reciprocal attraction of Jewish boys to Asian girls, es-tablishes Alpha Epsilon Pi as a safe, if exceptionally dull space of ethnic and cultural identity – but also a space in which Mark, sig-nificantly, makes a belated and reluctant entrance, lamenting the fact that this 'Caribbean' Night is decorated by a looped projection of Niagara Falls. As the film's opening dialogue suggests, Mark's fixation with Final Clubs seems largely based on his exclusion from them (and unlike in Mezrich's book, in the film we never even see him try to get in). But this, the film suggests, is only in part linked to his lack of athletic stature or a six-figure hedge fund.

Mark's thinly veiled jibe on hearing of his friend's initial success with the Phoenix Club is that it is 'probably a diversity thing'. His feigned insouciance here clashes with what he eagerly tells Erica earlier on in the Thirsty Scholar pub – that Final Clubs are sources of un-precedented 'access' and 'lead to a better life' – and his rejection of Eduardo later in the story seems driven at least in part by the fact that his friend had the temerity to successfully escape the confines of the Jewish fraternities, and in effect, to escape his own social and cultural designation as a Jew.

Not that Mark is in denial of his Jewish identity, however. Sorkin's fictionalized creation of Erica offers a version of the non-Jewish *shiksa* that, as Nathan Abrams points out, is a perennial object of desire for Jewish cinematic males (2012: 19). That Mark, subsequently, makes a dig at his ex's (possible) Germanic origins – 'Erica Albright is a bitch ... Perhaps that's because her family changed its name from A*lbrecht*' – strikes a chord with its historical, ethnic connotations.[4] And as much as Mark seems to be enthralled by Final Clubs, and frustrated with the trappings of Jewish identity at Harvard, he is still positioned antagonistically between two camps. Cameron and Tyler's patrician pledge to 'rehabilitate' Mark's social standing through his work on Harvard Connection appears to trigger Mark's determination to reverse their fortunes (and notably, on the fake 'Cameron Winklevoss' profile Zuckerberg set up on the Winklevoss's ConnectU site, he listed Cameron's hair colour as 'Aryan blond' (Carlson 2012)). The invention of Facebook, in this respect – proudly identified on its pages as 'A Mark Zuckerberg production' – is coded as much as an act of ethnic or cultural revenge as it is a purely personal one. When, in fact, Mark finally puts the site online, his rhythmic bobbing in front of the computer prompts Eduardo to ask whether he is 'praying', though Mark's movements more specifically connote the Jewish practice of *davening*, rather than Christian prayer – as Eduardo, presumably, would recognize.

One of *The Social Network*'s broader impacts, in this respect, is to add to a reconsideration of Jewishness on the American screen in the new millennium, and in this case, with a specific attention to youth. For Abrams, the most notable cinematic manifestation of this Jewish 'turn' is in those films written, directed or produced by Judd Apatow just prior to the production of *The Social Network*, such as *Superbad, Knocked Up*, and *The 40 Year-Old Virgin*. The ubiquity and popularity of these films, and the types of actors and characters populating them, suggests for Abrams a cultural normalization of young Jews (or at least male ones) in US cinema. *The Social Network* shows a form of continuity within that cinematic trend, though an important inflection here is the entrepreneurial and intellectual contexts within which *The Social Network* situates its Jewish characters. In effect – and, I would suggest, importantly – the film makes a claim for the 'geek' as a distinctively *Jewish* figure otherwise naturalized and co-opted by mainstream American culture. Mark's cinematic predecessors here would therefore broaden to include characters such as David Lightman, the computing whiz played by Jewish actor Matthew Broderick in *WarGames* (Badham 1983), who manages to hack into NORAD's defence system (Broderick 2007: 38–9; Shary 2005: 73–4); or indeed, the same actor's incarnation as the exemplary geek-entrepreneur in

Ferris Bueller's Day Off. For *The Social Network* to hint at this connection between Mark and earlier Jewish characters might seem an unnecessarily limiting or parochial one on the part of the film, until one recalls the more systemic – and, it is implied, in the allusions to Final Club exclusivity and tokenistic attention to diversity, vaguely anti-Semitic – hierarchies and divisions persisting at the time of Facebook's conception and development, at least in Sorkin's/Mark's vision of it.

Cameron and Tyler's role in the film is in part to embody what Leonardo Goi (2018) calls the 'antiquated 1.0 humans' whose contemporary relevance and claims to power are undermined by the 'Generation 2.0', represented by Mark, Sean and their peers at Facebook. At the same time, *The Social Network* focuses on the way that 'Human 1.0' is more specifically linked to the older networks of capital and business, but with the added suggestion that these are informed by particular *cultural* networks. Mezrich's (admittedly fictionalized) account in *The Accidental Billionaires*, for instance, is explicit in its emphasis on how the structures of judgement informing Harvard's hierarchical societies might be shaped by cultural, for which we might also read ethnic, prejudices. Or at least – and this is the film's broader point – that the Old-Money networks of Human 1.0 do not really recognize or accept the value of the geek, a figure that *The Social Network* provides with an ethnic and cultural inflection linking back to prior films. In a sequence not used in Sorkin's script, Mezrich fatefully allows the social assessment of Zuckerberg to be made, in the book's free-indirect style, partly by Saverin, watching on as both he and Mark try to make inroads at the Phoenix 'prepunch party':

> There was no way a kid like that was ever going to get into the Phoenix. A kid like that had no business punching any of the Final Clubs – God only knew what he had been doing at the prepunch party in the first place. Harvard had plenty of little niches for kids like that ... and hobbies catering to every imaginable twist of social impairment. One look at the kid, and it had been obvious to Eduardo that he didn't know the first thing about the sort of social networking one had to master to get into a club like the Phoenix. (Mezrich 2009: 9)

Mark's eventual meeting with Cameron, Tyler and Divya (Narendra) in the Porcellian 'Bicycle Room' consequently brings into play the film's established tensions since this holding room represents both the gateway to Mark's frustrated ambitions *and* the point beyond which he literally cannot go. Fincher neatly shoots the scene around firmly divided schematic lines, with the twins and Divya shot separately from Mark, who is positioned nearer the door to the street. Cameron passes Mark a compensatory sandwich: a nominally inclusive gesture that also confers a kind of serfdom, in a social order that need not be explained, because it is deemed to be self-evident ('You understand we can't take you past the bike room', Tyler tells, rather than asks, Mark).

Richard Brody (2010) has gone so far as to suggest that Sorkin's script revisits an older foundational myth about America and its popular cultural forms: in this case, as noted in the Introduction, one about the invention of Hollywood – an empire built by Jewish entrepreneurs in the early decades of the twentieth century. 'In order to assimilate into an America that hardly wanted them', Brody writes, these Jews 'transformed America by transforming America's images of itself'. Or as F. Scott Fitzgerald memorably put it, in the notes for what became his (unfinished) novel *The Last Tycoon* (1941), Hollywood 'is a Jewish holiday, a gentiles [sic] tragedy' (quoted in Brody 2010). In the same way, *The Social Network* is a Jewish revenge story of sorts about reshaping the world in one's image; only in this instance, the focus is less on the (presumed) slight inflicted on Mark by Erica, and more on that perpetrated by Cameron and Tyler, the moment they made Mark their vassal, offering him a sandwich and promising, in Divya's words, to 'rehabilitate [his] image'. Did this actually happen? Probably not, but biographical accuracy here is secondary to the potency of the story as a fable of American life, and of the life of the young especially: one in which a social misfit 'transfigures the world in such a way as to make him its king', becoming in the process no longer the serf, dependent on favours of the mighty, but himself 'the admired and feared and respected' (Brody 2010).

Education 2.0

It is this aspect of Mark's character that most clearly distinguishes him within the historical terms of the cinematic geek since for the most part this figure *expects* the subservient role. At the very least, if this status is a cause for dissatisfaction – in (fantastical, compensatory) films such as *Revenge of the Nerds*, or in *Weird Science* – the response, as already noted, is simply to find alternative ways to achieve the same goals as the geek's oppressors (Driscoll 2011: 49). As Shary argues, an exceptional case such as Brian (Anthony Michael Hall) in *The Breakfast Club*, who explicitly identifies as the geek within the film's cross-sectional group, achieves 'a certain independence' unavailable to the rest of the characters, precisely by not conforming to the conventions of heterosexual pairing we see at the film's conclusion (Shary 2005: 70). Brian embodies the model of 'intelligent empathy' that *The Breakfast Club*'s narrative as a whole encourages (Driscoll 2011: 49), and he becomes in both literal and cinematic terms (through his voiceover) the designated spokesperson for the group, and therefore the film. Nevertheless, in the end, his acceptance of his geek label, via his willingness to do everyone's detention essay for them, effectively leaves social hierarchies unquestioned and unchallenged: his independence is more a negotiation of the limited options available to him within these particular social contexts than it is a transcendence of them.

As both Shary (2005) and Broderick (2007) have observed, the same contexts of the 1980s saw an emerging subset of the youth film, in the form of movies about teens and 'tech': from the aforementioned *WarGames* and *Weird Science* to other films such as *The Last Starfighter* (Castle 1984), *Real Genius* (Coolidge 1985), *The Manhattan Project* (Brickman 1986) and *Space Camp* (Winer 1986). Such films, argues Shary, were an attempt on the part of Hollywood studios to engage with the growing prominence of computers and related technologies, especially videogames, in American life and youth culture especially. Shary locates these films as part of a broader spectrum of youth film, in which teen culture is exploited by studios, via films that at once feed off but ultimately defuse such culture's disruptive power. *WarGames*, in fact, in which the young hacker accidentally brings the world to the brink of nuclear war, epitomizes the type of 'teen tech' plot in which youthful scientific knowledge and creativity eventually 'threaten adult culture', and even (in this instance) Western civilization itself (Shary 2005: 72). Intelligence is celebrated in such films, but only 'until that intelligence becomes too problematic to even promote' (73); at which point, as in *WarGames*, we see a cooperation between the young protagonists and the more adult forces of authority and order. As both Shary and Broderick identify, it is through these resolutions that films such as *WarGames* and *The Manhattan Project* become more ambiguous in their treatment of youth, inasmuch as adolescent ingenuity might save the day, but only by solving a problem that adolescent curiosity triggers in the first place.

It is, then, *The Social Network*'s focus on (teen) technology that reinforces its significance within the youth film's wider field, though in many respects, it goes much further than these other films. This is because *The Social Network* resists *any* idea of the adult world – one that, as Mark in the film reiterates, cannot really understand what the younger protagonists are doing anyway – intervening in its business.

As noted previously, Fincher and Sorkin's film provides no negotiating or paternalistic adult influence: no one, for instance, acts as a check to the company's progress or the implications of its expansion (indeed, in terms of adult investors like the venture-capitalist Peter Thiel, depicted briefly in the film, their scale of investment effectively encourages unchecked growth). Concluding his survey of teen tech films, Shary suggests that this sub-genre has become overlooked by a predominant focus on consumption as a subject, rather than education, and an abiding fixation with delinquency and sex; leading him to speculate in 2005 that 'films about adolescents' intellectual or creative endeavors will continue to gain little notice' (Shary 2005: 76). Arguably, *The Social Network*'s ambivalent commitment to documenting its young protagonists' intellectual and creative endeavours, without in this case the guiding or reconciliatory hand of adults, means that it bucks this general trend; offering in its place a depiction of what happens when youthful ideas, and those that dream them up, are allowed to run away with themselves.

It is notable the extent to which, in *The Social Network*, adults become even less conspicuous than they already are after the move to Palo Alto. The rare grown-ups on the brighter, more colourful West Coast, like Thiel, do not really count anyway, because they are in on the deal (that is why they live there, after all). Cambridge, on the other hand, with its contrastingly subdued, permanently wintry tones – one might think from the film, if otherwise unaware, that Harvard was located somewhere in the Arctic Circle – is dominated by the wrong kind of adults, and the wrong kind of students, who dress in any case like they really want to be adults (as President Summers remarks on his first sighting of Cameron and Tyler in his office, they look like they 'want to sell [him] a Brooks Brothers franchise'). If Harvard, as the film's schematic depiction suggests, represents a world in which you do not really belong, the ultimate revenge is simply to turn your back on it: not out of spite or lassitude, but more simply, because you do not need to stay. *The Social Network* might be ambivalent with regard to the significance of being at Harvard in the first instance, but the final jab it makes in the direction of Zuckerberg's *alma mater* is to suggest that, in the grander scheme of things – and above all, in the contexts of a world increasingly dictated by the young, digitally native and technologically gifted – it might even be an irrelevance.

As I have noted in this chapter, a constituent part of mainstream popular cinema, and perhaps of the youth film above all, is to provide a utopian, mythic dimension that can reconcile tensions, or dramatically conceal more prosaic realities. The youth film, with its perennial focus on the 'carnival' of high school- or college life, offers a form of idealized and suspended moment in time, often with a nostalgic dimension. To recall Driscoll's point, such films revel in their immaturity, providing in the process a joyful overturning of the social order (2011: 76–9); albeit one that, like the duration of the feature-length movie itself, can only be temporary, constrained by the reality of encroaching maturity and mundane, everyday responsibility. Symbolized by the bitter-sweet passage of graduation, maturity is the mostly unspoken but inevitable destination of films like, among many others, *Risky Business, Animal House* and *Ferris Bueller's Day Off.* That last film's book-ending mantra – 'Life moves pretty fast' – might be the take-home message of the film, yet it is only superficially affirmative, acknowledging in its own wording the inevitable entropy that is a part of later life, once youth has 'moved on'.

The significant intervention of *The Social Network* within these contexts is in effect to depict the creation of a technological alternative to such largely unchallenged educational settings: one, moreover, that is not constrained by the temporary passage of acquiring a high-school diploma or college degree, for which, in any case, there no longer seems to be such a need. 'I'm talking about taking the entire social experience of college and putting it online', says Mark, though in this case with no pre-determined end-date: 'it's like a Final Club except we're the president'.

The film's initial section at Harvard, with its display of gilded youth, would seem to offer the most utopian aspects of the youth film. Yet even here, the social, economic and also cultural hierarchies structuring experience within college ensure that this utopia is not so readily available on a universal scale. As I will consider in more detail in the following chapter, for Mark, his utopia is largely one engineered through code, and in the virtual zones and dispersed interactions of the Internet, less constrained by time, space and other material obstacles. For Mark and Sean, the party does not need to end. Immaturity, within *their* world at least, has no limits. And yet, as Mark reminds his litigants and both sets of lawyers, his version of utopian immaturity is written in a code that only he and his friends can truly manipulate. Mark, as Erica assures us at the top of the film, is an asshole. Whatever anyone says to the contrary, it is not clear he ever stops being one, or whether he really cares one way or the other. Like it or not – and in the end, this is at the heart of *The Social Network*'s ambiguities – the world in which most of the planet lives is one created in this asshole's brilliant image.

Notes

1 As Zuckerberg described it to the Harvard *Crimson*, 'We all just sat around one day, and were, like, "We're not going back to school are we? Nah"' (quoted in Levy 2020: 96).
2 A Treasury Secretary for President Bill Clinton, at the time of the film's production, Summers worked within the Obama administration as National Economic Council director.
3 Driscoll's reference to 'carnival' refers specifically to Mikhail Bakhtin's (1984) discussion of the term, seen as a temporary period of suspension and inversion of the social order in medieval society.
4 The beginning of Mark's blog-post, narrated in voiceover in *The Social Network*, is taken mostly verbatim from the quoted blog entries in Mezrich (2009: 42), though the name is removed in the latter account. The subsequent play on Erica's name seems to be Sorkin's own intervention.

2 Move Fast and Break Things: Ambivalences of Speed and Hacker Aesthetics

MARK: Did you know there are more people with genius IQs living in China than there are people of any kind living in the United States?

ERICA: That can't possibly be true.

MARK: It is.

So begins *The Social Network*; the conversation emerging, as Sorkin's screenplay stipulates, 'From the black', onto an establishing shot of Mark and Erica sitting opposite each other in the Thirsty Scholar pub. There is little time to adjust to the setting, or to ease ourselves into the film's environment. The film insists on our efforts to engage immediately, and above all, to listen. A lot is packed into the film's opening conversation; so much so that anyone spending the first few minutes of *The Social Network* arranging their popcorn, working out where to put the remote, or finding a comfortable position with their laptop, might well find themselves wondering what exactly is going on.

As media theorist Steven Johnson notes (2005: 75–7), Sorkin developed this deliberately estranging approach to dialogue while authoring *The West Wing* during its first four seasons. Frequently, in the type of 'cold open' that *The Social Network*'s opening scene echoes, *West Wing* episodes would begin with the fast-talking White House staff commenting on a situation to which we have no prior information. This was not itself new – the use of narratives starting like this *in media res* goes back at least to Shakespeare – but it *was* unusual at the time for a network television show. For Johnson, it is precisely the cognitive attention a show like *The West Wing* demands of its viewers that makes it so engaging. As has now become an assumption rather than an exception within long-form narrative television, *The West Wing* rewards its viewer's mental labour through complexity. It might

DOI: 10.4324/9781003161936-3

not necessarily make a viewer any smarter, as Johnson hints, but it might at least make them *feel* smarter for keeping up.

If one needs to keep up, the implication is that these characters must be clever, or at least a bit cleverer than the viewer. *The Social Network*, in turn, offers this similar suggestion. Can the dialogue be followed? If not, one needs to work it out. There is, though, an added dimension to the dialogue here, since viewers of *The Social Network* are not merely parsing information about the narrative world, but implied information about the protagonists themselves. It is hardly accidental, for instance, that the seemingly random anecdote with which *The Social Network* begins mentions the word 'genius', especially when the point of Mark's tale becomes clear:

MARK: But here's my question: How do you distinguish yourself in a population of people who all got 1600 on their SATs?
ERICA: I didn't know they take SATs in China.
MARK: They don't. I wasn't talking about China anymore, I was talking about me.

In other words, Mark is quickly at pains to remind his soon-to-be ex-girlfriend that the important genius IQ in this conversation does not belong to one of the many Chinese millions: it belongs to him.

Why does it matter? Is one supposed to be wowed by Mark's revelation? I do not think so, especially as Mark's initial factoid, as Erica so calmly suggests, is nonsense.[1] One effect of Sorkin and Fincher's opening scene is to establish the highly ambivalent position it takes with regard to its subjects: an ambivalence that is rarely encouraged in a show such as *The West Wing*. While it deploys the same techniques, the film invites reflection not just on how smart its protagonist might be, but what his intelligence is actually *for*. As I have already argued, one needs to reflect on what *The Social Network* ultimately suggests about its particular generation, and more specifically the culture, both shaping and shaped by Mark and his peers. I looked at this in the last chapter, with reference to the film's depiction of education. In this chapter, building on the last, I consider the extent to which the film's style is a contributing factor in these representational concerns.

Freakin' Fast: *The Social Network* and the Culture of Acceleration

A key aspect of understanding film style is to recognize how specific choices shape and inform narrative content. Film never merely presents a given story around which 'style' serves as an embellishment or optional extra. Inasmuch as style constitutes the set of technical and aesthetic choices any filmmaker makes from an array of options, and determines what is seen on screen and how, style and narrative are mostly inseparable. As David Bordwell and Kristin Thompson put it, every stylistic component within a film *'functions as part of the overall pattern* that is perceived' by the viewer (2004: 50, emphasis in the original). What might be 'known' from the narrative on screen can only be a result of the manipulations of style on the part of the filmmakers.

Equally, though, it is important to situate film style in terms of its specific historical contexts; and in this case, within the broader circumstances of global film industries, and Hollywood in particular. In the production contexts of a film like *The Social Network*, these questions of film aesthetics are, from some perspectives, not merely questions of an individual filmmaker preference (or what some might call 'auteur' style). In Hollywood cinema of the twenty-first century, stylistic choices have become the subject of an often highly evaluative critical debate, focusing above all on the perception of this cinema's increasing *speed*. Fincher and Sorkin's film came out around the same time as, in wider debates around film theory and practice, the perceived acceleration of contemporary film was becoming a target; especially from filmmakers and critics bewailing, as one commentator apocalyptically described it, 'the speed death of the eye' (Blackmore 2007; for a summary of these debates, see Kendall 2016). The perceived speed of modern films, and the rush of audio-visual data with which they bombard eye and ear, is from this point of view another symptom of a mass culture that denies time for contemplation, simply adding stimulus upon stimulus, with Hollywood the weapon of mass distraction at its centre.

One obvious criterion for this perceived acceleration of modern film is the rate at which such films are now edited. Bordwell, surveying Hollywood cinema since the 1960s and into the new century, has elaborated on what he calls modern Hollywood's 'intensified continuity' system (2006: 121–38); a central element of which is the incrementally decreasing average shot length (ASL) across these decades. Contemporaneously pacey films such as 1964s *Goldfinger*, with its ASL of 4.0 seconds, now seem sluggish when compared to Hollywood films of the early 2000s, many of which have an ASL of half that length (121–2). Importantly, Bordwell highlights that this is not just a tendency within certain types of film we might normally identify as 'fast', such as action films, but rather one spread across the range of Hollywood output, from children's animations to rom-coms (123).

This impression of increasing speed within a culture of increased media saturation, for its critics, epitomizes a culture of increased attention deficiency, and in narrative film terms, a tendency towards fragmentation and spatial incoherence. Most relevantly to the discussion of *The Social Network*, it is the cognitive shifts represented by the Internet, with its multiple windows, hyperlinks and perpetual alerts and notifications, that is for some a harbinger and vehicle of this same attention-deficient culture. For digital skeptics such as Nicholas Carr, author of the 2008 article 'Is Google Making Us Stupid?' (subsequently developed into his 2011 book *The Shallows*), the tremendous width of information offered by the Internet and its search engines, while offering a superficial benefit in terms of scope and knowledge, is offset by a resultant loss of *depth*. As Carr argues, the organizational structure of the Internet, and computing more broadly, with its tendency towards ceaseless movement and visual replenishment, is effectively (re)shaping the wiring of our brains. Advanced developments in media technologies, says Carr, have encouraged our original, prehistoric tendencies towards 'distractedness'; our 'predisposition ... to shift our gaze, and hence our attention, from one object to the other' (2011: 63). Such 'fast-paced, reflexive shifts in focus' were vital for our ancestors' survival in an environment of predators and food scarcity, but these were qualities our *civilized* minds – along with the development of an oral culture, and later the invention of the book – no longer required. 'To read a book' was by contrast 'to practice an unnatural process of thought, one that demanded sustained, unbroken attention to a single, static object' (64).

In cinematic terms, one might see this 'sustained, unbroken attention' in terms of the comparatively sedate and coherent forms of the classical Hollywood style, and the long take in particular – an increasingly marginalized device in mainstream cinema, and entirely absent in Fincher and Sorkin's film. By contrast, *The Social Network* appears to offer viewers units of information, and a persistent shifting of attention.[2] Its opening scene, while the longest in the film, still provides a case in point in terms of the way it is edited. One of the questions engaging practitioners and analysts of film editing throughout history is the notion of *appropriate* shot length. As editor and theorist Walter Murch suggested (writing originally in the early 1990s), editing corresponds to the notion of a thought or phrase. 'The sequence of thoughts', argues Murch, 'that is, the rhythm and rate of cutting ... should be appropriate to whatever the audience is watching'. Notably, though, Murch relies on a quite genre-determined notion of what such 'appropriate' rhythm and rate ought to be:

'Depending on how it is staged, a convincing action sequence might have around twenty-five cuts a minute, whereas a dialogue scene would still feel "normal" ... averaging six cuts per minute or less' (Murch 2001: 68–9). *Six cuts per minute?* Murch here suggests an ASL of ten seconds, extremely slow by comparison with Bordwell's suggested figures across recent Hollywood films. Oddly enough, then, when we look at *The Social Network*'s opening sequence in detail, we find that the five-minute scene has 116 shots: in other words, just under 'twenty-five cuts a minute'. Yet this is for a conversation sequence, shot around a table, featuring entirely static characters. In other words, within Murch's terms, Fincher shoots Sorkin's opening dialogue as if it were an action sequence.

Does this, then, represent everything 'bad' about twenty-first-century Hollywood? In a book on that same subject, Wheeler Dixon and Gwendolyn Foster suggest that it probably does. Besides their casual put-down of *The Social Network* ('a handsomely mounted TV movie – linear, easy to follow, bereft of nuance or subtlety' (2011: 33)), Dixon and Foster's book opens with the speculative assertion that Hollywood's increasingly faster editing rates are part of an overall aesthetic strategy 'designed to keep audiences in a dazzled stupor' (7). Interestingly, though, some of the more specific evidence they employ offers a potentially very different view of such aesthetic approaches, particularly when they highlight how cutting rates and types of shot distribution seem designed to reflect growing tendencies in Western culture towards 'visual multitasking'. Cinematic vision, they suggest, 'has fallen into line with human vision ... cinematic shot structure has grown ever more hyperkinetic and fragmented, just as an actual observer might confront such a scene in real life' (49). Rather than see this as an inevitable symptom of audience attention-deficiency, I suggest here that these circumstances be viewed in terms of their mimetic possibilities for representing these same human visual contexts – the very contexts giving rise to the emergence of Facebook.

Let the Hacking Begin

In an ultimately more ambivalent response to the question of contemporary cinematic speed, Steven Shaviro has noted what he sees as the move away from spatial and narrative coherence, and even from cinematic 'continuity' itself, in favour of a more programmatic and commercially-calculated 'moment-by-moment manipulation of the spectator's affective state' (2010: 118). Speed, in conjunction with montage, is hardly a new development: the 'shock effect' of juxtaposing sequences of images, often in quick succession, was a hallmark, for instance, of Soviet cinema from the silent era, in films like Dziga Vertov's *Man with a Movie Camera* (1929), or Sergei Eisenstein's *Battleship Potemkin* (1925). The difference now, as Shaviro sees it, is that this effect carries no narrative, ideological or conceptual force, but is deployed rather to 'generate a maximum audience response', in the form of 'excitement' (120). Shaviro's own (political) view on what he calls the aesthetics of 'accelerationism' is that it can be used to 'exhaust' or 'disrupt' the same capitalist media institutions and ideologies that produced such forms, essentially by becoming as fast and fragmented as humanly possible (137). While I agree with Shaviro's sense that filmmakers might use the accelerated aesthetics of contemporary film to reflect upon or critique an accelerated contemporary culture, my slightly different argument here focuses on the way *The Social Network* employs speed to lay bare not just the deliriously fast contexts both informing and reinforced by Facebook's creation but also its (negative) impacts: what, in short, is broken in this same process.

As Lisa Purse has remarked, commentators confronting the speed of recent cinema, lamenting for a lost sense of visual 'intelligibility', 'spatial integrity' and 'orientation' – all hallmarks of classical narrative cinema's continuity system – over-evaluate these same qualities as both representational and ontological (2016: 152–3). Purse suggests, in turn, we acknowledge the *transforming* perceptual contexts in which we find ourselves, or the 'other kinds of aesthetic principles' shaped by and responding to experiences that, for good or bad, cannot be nostalgically corralled within classical paradigms (153). Rather, then, than thinking of the stylistic approaches in *The Social Network* as being at variance with 'appropriate' form and patterns, this chapter asks what it is that makes the film's style appropriate for its subject matter. In what way, in other words, do the contexts, the meaning and the narrative of *The Social Network* find their most suitable form in the film's stylistic system, and why is this an appropriate form for a film focusing on, and potentially speaking to, youth?

In a feature on Sorkin and *The Social Network*, Mark Harris draws attention to the screenwriter's authorial obsession with pace, and more specifically,

the remorseless hyperspeed of the communications profession. [Sorkin's dialogue is] the sound of characters whose minds and mouths work faster than those of the people around them, guys whose conversational aesthetic is, in Fincher's phrase, "about the absolute total tonnage of words". (Harris 2010)

The final point here is key, highlighting as it does that, in the mouths of *The Social Network*'s young protagonists, Sorkin's verbal gymnastics have a *quantitative* dimension. As noted earlier, the film at once exploits and relishes the effects of speed, while also hinting at some of its drawbacks, such as the incapacity for reflection, or the tendency towards superficiality.

The opening dialogue offers a case in point. While the film looks to whip viewers along with its breathtaking pace of exchange, in terms of content, the conversation itself shows two characters entirely at odds with each other, frequently miscommunicating, their questions and responses disconnected or lacking association. Fincher and his editors (Angus Wall and Kirk Baxter) underline these points by never, apart from at the beginning, and during an awkward pause in the middle, showing the two characters within the same medium shot, restricting them instead to single close-ups. Indeed, what is this 'couple' even talking *about*? Mark's opening nugget about China's genius IQs is, dare we say it, precisely an example of the kind of 'fake news' which Facebook, in recent years, has been criticized with helping to propagate. Mark's response to Erica's doubts ('It is') merely asserts what he assumes to be the accuracy of his own empty claim. But so what? Even if it were true, it is a hollow assertion, the kind of callow utterance that only someone so hyped by their sense of intellectual superiority might choose to brandish. It happens so fast, though, that without more time to consider it, one might take it as a given (there are, after all, a lot of people in China). The problem is that in a culture of acceleration, does one have the time to think?[3]

The degree to which the film highlights this fact, though, illustrates the way speed – its excitement, *and* its shallowness – becomes a part of the film's narrative subject matter, not simply its 'style'. As I have argued elsewhere (Archer 2016), while 'fast talking' may be perceived as simply another symptom of contemporary cinema's ever-increasing drive to acceleration, its use also evokes the type of dialogue at work in classical Hollywood genres such as the journalist film and screwball comedy. In such films, speech can become a weapon or a deliberate source of confusion; just as here, the dialogue allows for reflection on the very problems and deceptions of (fast) speech itself. The speed of thought and speech coming from Mark conveys its own sense of entitlement and privilege, carried along by the assumption of the right to speak, and the assumption that what is said is somehow worth saying (and note how, until the end, it is Erica – who as Mark patronisingly notes later, 'go[es] to B.U.' – who tends to stumble in the face of Mark's insistent verbal barrage). But it is the same velocity and abruptly shifting, *superficial* nature of Mark's speech that also might alert a viewer to its emptiness and lack of moral and intellectual centre.

In 2009, Facebook designer Ben Barry put up a series of poster slogans around the company's new offices on California Avenue, one of them simply stating 'Move Fast and Break Things'; a phrase that, for a time, became Facebook's 'unofficial motto' (Levy 2020: 241). Over the years, moving fast and breaking things would become an uncomfortable description of Facebook's more ill-considered actions and their repercussions, but in 2009 it was a statement of intent; a reiteration of Zuckerberg's belief that 'Facebook's edge came from its speed and risk-taking. Going slow would mean death' (243). Acceleration, then, in all its ambiguity, is the virus permeating *The Social Network*, even its very point, and trying to find a way to encompass this ambiguity becomes the work of the film's aesthetic system.

Speed, indeed, permeates every aspect of the film's narrative. The creation of Facemash draws attention not because it is a beautiful creation (it is not) but because it crashes a Harvard university network unable to contend with the speed of traffic it generates. Note how Marylin (Rashida Jones), the assistant lawyer at Mark's depositions, is amazed most of all not by the fact that Facemash received 22,000 hits, but that it got these *in two hours*. The viral impact of Facemash in turn thematically foreshadows the film's ensuing focus on Facebook's rapid expansion and take up, but also the way in which the film is about competing regimes of speed. Mark's race to get Facebook across US campuses is a race in part to pre-empt and dominate Cameron, Tyler and Divya, and it is one of the serendipitous aspects of the Facebook story that Cameron and Tyler should also be elite rowers, future Olympians, their lives defined by the imperative to come first ('Those guys are freakin' *fast!*' murmurs an awed rower on the Charles River, in the film's first sighting of the twins). Note too how Eduardo's later betrayal at the Facebook offices, and his bitter face-off with Mark, happens in sight of an enormous totalizer, clicking through ever-increasing numbers on the way to Facebook's first million members, as well as Sean's promised billion-dollar payoff.

As hinted here, speed, both as an idea and in its connection to competition, is intrinsic to the dramatic structure and dynamics of *The Social Network*. Rebecca Sheehan has gone so far as to describe the film as a 'tragedy' of speed, with Mark a character 'subject to and guilty of realizing information too late to act on it' (2013: 37). But to add to Sheehan's point, *The Social Network* is also structured around the consequences of saying or writing things that become instantly part of the world, their damage already done in the flash of a thought or press of a keyboard button: telling Erica she cannot possibly need to study because she goes to an inferior college, or then calling her 'a bitch' on the Internet; launching Facemash while drunk on beer and spite; taunting the Harvard Connection team via emails that come back as evidence in litigation. *Move fast and break things* might be the motto of Facebook, but the characters in *The Social Network* abide by a slightly different code: *Act first, think later.*

Speed is as much the *problem*, then, as merely the subject represented in Fincher and Sorkin's film. To come back to Purse's point, though, in spite of its preoccupations with extreme pace, *The Social Network* rarely sacrifices 'intelligibility' (and this, I would suggest, is why Dixon and Wheeler's objections to the film's 'linearity' are inconsistent with their broader complaint about Hollywood, since the *absence* of clarity seems to be part of a wider problem they identify). The first scene is once again a good case in point here since it is constructed very strictly in line with the principles of classical continuity editing, with its shot–reverse shot form, fixed cameras and adherence to the 180° rule.[4] As with this same scene's use of extremely short ASLs (as noted earlier), the film's general impact derives not from its abandonment, but from its intensified manipulation of continuity style.

Another example is the extended sequence in which Mark hacks into the Harvard house facebooks, while a party at the Phoenix – real, or imagined, simultaneous or otherwise, it is not actually clear – plays out at the same (screen) time. At one moment, we see Mark fleetingly in close-up before his computer, a green plastic dart in his mouth, as the breakneck voiceover of his hacking blog plays out: 'Lowell has some security. They require a username/password combo ...'. The action subsequently cuts to a slightly slowed, reverse tracking shot of girls, fresh off the bus, entering through a set of double doors; before a return to Kirkland shows, in extreme close-up, a window on Mark's laptop asking authentication for access to the Lowell facebook (Figure 2.1). There is a quick return to the previous tracking shot, as a club member leads one of the girls in, while two other boys in the background check out the new female arrivals (Figure 2.2); before going back again to the Lowell window on Mark's laptop, where another authentication code is typed in (Figure 2.3). A medium shot of Mark with his roommates behind him is then followed by two more almost subliminal shots of the computer screen, before the sequence returns to a shot of the Phoenix bar, while at the same time we hear the continuation of the voiceover ('... I'm going to go ahead and say they

Figure 2.1 An extreme close-up of Mark's hacking...

Figure 2.2 ...interrupts a slowed tracking shot from the Phoenix...

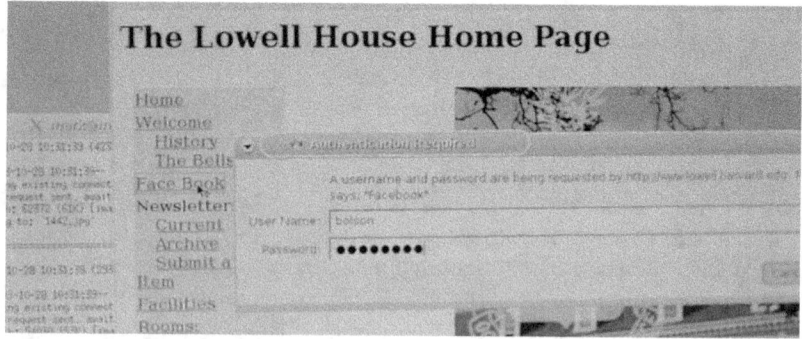

Figure 2.3 ...and then returns to the next stage of the hacking.

don't have access to main FAS user database, so they have no way of detecting an intrusion').

This whole sequence of nine shots lasts just under ten seconds: an ASL of 1.1. The sequence picks up again slightly later, as now, the girls, along with more of the members, and again shot in a slowed tracking shot, are moving and dancing through the rooms. Interspersed within this same fluid shot are more close-ups approximately coinciding with Mark's continued voiceover: a shot of a blog entry being successfully posted; a window of the Quincy House webpage partially masking one of the hacked facebooks; a side-angle shot of Mark's hands tapping away at the keyboard. The entire first part of this broader sequence in the film, from Mark's initiation of the project ('It's on ...') to the brief hiatus when Eduardo arrives, lasts two and a half minutes and contains just over a hundred shots: a remarkably fast ASL of 1.5 seconds.

For all its pace and insistent movement back-and-forth between locations, though, there is no loss of either 'intelligibility', 'spatial integrity' or 'orientation' here; not even if one chooses to see the Phoenix party figures as imagined, since they still represent a form of motivation or target for Mark's activities. The style here, rather, offers more of a bridge between an 'accelerated' aesthetics and a classical form of montage and continuity style that encourages an anchored perception and comprehension of what is being viewed. At the same time, the scene links both mimetically and thematically to the film's broader interests in velocity and the transformed spatiality of Internet culture. Michele Schreiber identifies how the film here depicts a form of restructuring in terms of the social order; one that the film, as a product of digital filmmaking culture itself, 'both shows and enacts' (Schreiber 2016: 4).[5] For example, the way that the editing here effectively 'hacks' into the continuous tracking shots of the Phoenix Club sequence is in its own way a hallmark of intensified continuity style, taking advantage of digital film stock and editing tools to manipulate classical cinematic form and shot construction. 'While [classical Hollywood] directors avoided cutting in the middle of a camera movement, today's filmmakers feel no hesitation' argues Bordwell: 'now track[ing shots] and pans are usually interrupted by cuts, denying us a sense of steady progression' (Bordwell 2006: 123). In other words, filmmaking within the classical era – shot on film, and edited by hand – more frequently respected the integrity and indivisibility of the camera movement from A to B: by contrast, the fragmentation of the tracking shot in *The Social Network* purposely *disrupts* this integrity of classical form. Yet here, such disruption is never just for its own sake, but is clearly allied to what it narrates, since it *virtually* represents the way in which Mark's hacking penetrates the parameters and protocols of Final Club exclusivity, both figuratively and imaginatively.

The same tracking shots of the Phoenix party, in a very different film – one, for instance, about these clubs in themselves – would have a very different value, charged, perhaps, with the energy of the young people dancing and moving through the space. By interrupting these very shots, though, the impact is different, since it shifts the point of view through which they might be seen, subordinating them to Mark's activity at the computer. Indeed, as Sheehan has pointed out, the very ambiguity of the Phoenix images in terms of their provenance carries its own representative and metaphorical value within the 'cultural instantaneity' of our contemporary moment, especially in the era of blogging, posting and tweeting. The reality of these images, Sheehan suggests, 'doesn't matter'; rather, 'the interchange between fantasy and reality depicted through this intercutting is similar to the relationship with reality established by Facebook: the power of the mediated representation (particularly as it gains quick circulation) becomes such that it degrades the real' (2013: 41–2). The image, instantly transmissible, 'performs like the real until it is indistinguishable from reality' (42).

No less significantly, the sequence here also inscribes the encroachment of a 'new media' aesthetics, or as I would put it, a form of 'digital realism' into mainstream narrative form. As Lev Manovich has argued, the material and perceptual properties of software and computers have transformed our relationship to visual culture. The computer as a visual interface both manifests and normalizes formerly 'avant-garde aesthetic strategies' such as collage, once conceivable only in terms of experimental film traditions: 'what used to be exceptions for traditional cinema [have become] the normal, intended techniques of digital film-making, embedded in technology design itself' (Manovich 2002: 413). One might note, for example, how in this same sequence from *The Social Network* the traditional work of cinematic editing – the organization of changing shots in a sequence – is at points usurped by the refreshing or layering, within the non-edited shot, of the computer screen's 'windows' themselves, with Mark, via his laptop, effectively taking the place of the editor within the sequence's diegesis. Indeed, Manovich observes that the cinema's 'rectangular framing of representational reality' is a format shared by the computer screen's interface (2001: 88). The result is that the computer becomes a kind of cinema – and, potentially, vice versa – only with a different type of 'reality' being represented: 'The window in a fictional world of a cinematic narrative has become a window in a datascape' (92).

The computer screen *is* a cinema screen – one which, in turn, becomes a new kind of world.

As touched on above, this same sequence also maps out in broader film-historical terms the replacement of a particular idea of *action*. While in the Thirsty Scholar scene one might understand 'action' in terms of the speed of thought and response, in the Facemash sequence, action is partly removed from direct human activity itself, mediated by the windows of the computer screen. The idea, reinforced in *The Social Network*, that such a reconfiguration of action is linked to particular *generational* shifts in both film and the wider culture is further highlighted one year after *The Social Network* in *Moneyball* (Miller 2011), co-written by Sorkin, adapted from Michael Lewis's non-fiction book (2003). Centring on the fortunes of the Oakland A's baseball team during one extraordinary season, the film explores the process through which the team's general manager, drawing on the programming talents of his young, geeky, Ivy League-graduate assistant, Peter Brand, selects players not by the way they look but by what their metrics reveal about them.[6]

In one sequence, for instance, Brand shows his boss the process through which data analysis software can pinpoint the most effective players within the limited price range available to his team. As in the comparable sequence from *The Social Network*, the computer screen here absorbs the extent of the cinematic frame, providing an editing logic dictated largely by Brand's own algorithms and inputs. Subtle re-positionings in the image between shots, in the form of new windows, re-framings or push-in cuts, shift our attention from scrolls of information to specific data. From the initial waves of computer code and statistics *en masse*, the camera eventually moves towards selected mathematical formulae, and eventually, in extreme close-up, to the figure of '$237,000': the going price for Chad Bradford, an overlooked pitcher with a 'funny' underarm action, valued by Brand at ten times the going price. The ASL here is around two seconds, putting the sequence at the extreme edge of Bordwell's 'intensified' continuity spectrum. Yet, like Mark in *The Social Network*, Brand has not even got out of his chair this whole time. In a film preoccupied with how appearances are misjudged, physical prowess here means little: in order to change his world, Brand, like Mark, does not even need to move.

In the previous chapter, I noted how the youthful hackers and gamers of 'tech'-oriented teen film typically find themselves re-integrated within the adult world. Rarely, though, do these earlier-generation teens get to run or radically transform the system. By contrast, as Schreiber points out, more recent films like *The Social Network*,

Moneyball, or *Up in the Air* (Reitman 2009), in which Anna Kendrick's youthful innovator devises a means of firing employees online, thereby rendering her middle-aged, frequent-flier counterpart (George Clooney) himself redundant, hint towards a changing technocentric worldview; one in which 'the rise of technology goes hand in hand with the increasing vulnerability of established systems of power' (Schreiber 2016: 11). Schreiber situates these films, including *The Social Network*, within the contexts of the global economic recession (from 2008 onwards) in the backdraft of which they were all made; a recession, she argues, that was from a sociological perspective as much a 'he-cession', given that it was the traditionally male, blue-collar jobs that took the biggest brunt. These films are pointed, then, in the way they depict 'an older generation of men's corporeal and often tangible conceptions of labor – building products and establishing solid, mutually respectful business relationships – in the process of being replaced by a new [technological] modus operandi' (ibid.). Not everyone, of course, will lose out in this process: algorithms and automation might slowly render many humans redundant, but in the process, and in the true spirit of disruption – where those who can, do so simply because it is there to be done – 'wealth and power might become concentrated in the hands of the tiny elite that owns the[se] all-powerful algorithms' (Harari 2015: 376).

What is effectively seen then in *The Social Network* is an aesthetic enacting of the processes through which this specifically young digital elite disrupts established power. There is, in turn, a synthesis and reciprocity between the impacts of new digital tools (what is narratively represented in the film) and the very tools themselves (the *means* through which this narrative is represented). Through the combined effects of the editing, moving between the locations and actions on screen, it is as if the happy, laughing party-goers at the Phoenix are unaware of being narratively and culturally usurped by the tools of this new emerging technocracy. As Schreiber highlights, what is at stake here in this digital takeover is the power of older, masculine bodies, representatives of an 'analog' era, and their vulnerability to the intrusions both of Mark's actions, along with the social and economic transformations of digital culture more generally. Insofar as the members of the Phoenix mostly approximate the type of masculine bodies that Mark associates with Final Clubs – jocks, or guys who 'row crew' – these bodies exemplify an image of dominant masculine strength, linked here to erstwhile structures of power. As noted earlier, though, these bodies are increasingly 'under threat of diminishment', at the hands of less agile and less physically prepossessing, but more 'intellectually driven bodies': the ones that, crucially, are increasingly 'in control of technology' (Schreiber 2016: 4).

The Sounds of Speed

The persistent voiceover on the soundtrack during this same sequence, which is heard at the expense of the diegetic sound from the Phoenix, is an intriguing choice, given some of its more negative associations in the theory of film aesthetics. Screenwriting guru Robert McKee, most famously, has been vociferous in his distrust of much voiceover narration, going so far as to say it *'threatens the future of our art'* (1998: 344, emphasis in the original). Badly used voiceover, in McKee's view, disrespects its audience through its tendency to explain, thereby diminishing the potential ambiguities of the image and the capacity of an audience to infer meaning (345). While it works here as a shorthand access to the content of Mark's blog, which would otherwise need to be displayed at length on the screen, one of the potential redundancies of its use here is that it often reiterates the same words presented on screen, albeit briefly, in terms of what Mark is typing.

Voiceover in film is not a uniform technique but has different effects in relation to what is simultaneously visualized. Voiceover is always by definition 'asynchronous' with the film image since it lies outside the immediate diegesis of the action (Kozloff 1988: 103). This sequence from *The Social Network* is no exception since what we hear on the soundtrack has no *literal* relationship to anything happening within the actual world of the film (Mark is not actually speaking out loud), but merely *corresponds* to the words Mark is typing in his blog. The specific quality and contribution of voiceover depends on its varying degree of 'redundancy', as film terminology would put it, with regard to the visual narration. A high level of redundancy would see the vocal track effectively relating what is visible and intelligible on the screen; what Sarah Kozloff terms 'overlapping' voiceover (104). Just as often, though, voiceover has a 'complementary' quality, insofar as the words spoken on the soundtrack add something to the understanding of the image, and vice versa: such 'complementary pairings', writes Kozloff, 'provide more information than would have been available from either [voiceover or image] alone. New knowledge is created by the juxtaposition of the two' (106).

The significant point in *The Social Network* is the extent to which the connection between voiceover and image is disrupted with the addition of the Phoenix party shots, and in turn, how the film generates the kinds of ambiguity often denied by overlapping voiceover narration. The parallel of word and image here *implies* a connection and production of meaning one might find oneself working to create, in the mode of complementary voiceover. Kozloff compares the work of such voiceover to what the Soviet director and film-theorist Sergei Eisenstein called 'vertical montage' (ibid.), in which two otherwise disparate images and ideas combine, sometimes metaphorically, to create powerful new associations in the viewer's mind. In this sequence, the intelligibility of what we are seeing, in the form of the Phoenix Club images, is offset by the incessant intrusion of Mark's hacking blog and the processes he recounts. Voiceover here asserts a level of control over the visual information. A related effect of this technique, as we have seen, is to turn the otherwise active subjects of the Phoenix party into seemingly manipulable *objects* of Mark's actions.

Moreover, and significantly for the concerns of this book, the film's use of voiceover here is again specifically generational, in its mimetic appeal to various levels and channels of simultaneous digital-media activity. I have already noted the importance of speed in terms of the intelligibility of dialogue, but the additional value here is the *dispersion* of the vocal track across sometimes complementary, though in other respects competing, visual information. In a scene following the Facemash sequence, Divya will highlight the fact that Mark was hacking the house facebooks, writing the code for Facemash, while also 'blogging simultaneously' – all the while being drunk. Divya's subsequent response that 'this is our guy' only underlines the point that Mark's high-performance multi-tasking is the specific ability they are looking for. It is the same capacity to spread attention and cognitive faculties across multiple platforms of information and activity which is viewed – depending on one's position – as either the most liberating or damaging feature of our Internet and digital culture. As Johnson suggests, echoing the earlier point that Facebook is born of young Internet denizens raised on AOL Instant Messenger:

> The accelerating pace of new platforms and software applications forces users to probe and master new environments. Your mind is engaged by the interactive content of networked media – posting a response to an article online, maintaining three separate IM conversations at the same time – but you're also exercising cognitive muscles interacting with the *form* of the media as well. (2005: 121–2)

In the same way that Sorkin's dialogue encourages its audience to play a game of catch-up, *The Social Network* seems also to challenge viewers to keep up in a *lateral* and s*patial* sense, reflecting the multiple, simultaneous areas of attention with which its main protagonist engages. Whether of course so much content is *worth* keeping up with, morally or intellectually speaking, is a moot point, but this is consistent with the film's own ambivalences towards its subject matter. As Carr argues, implicitly taking issue with Johnson's more utopian conclusions, the 'visual-spatial intelligence' developed through our use of the Internet and the plethora of other screen-based technologies is a limited one, since such 'intelligence' is ultimately 'define[d] by the Net's own standards' (2011: 141). In other words, the Internet might be making us smarter, but only if getting smarter means finding our way more quickly around the Internet and its related platforms and applications. *The Social Network*'s blunter position on this point is that, for the denizens of Facebook, *it doesn't matter*, since the kind of 'deep' reading abilities and contemplative, long-term reasoning skills Carr advocates are superfluous to the immediate and instantaneous requirements of Web 2.0 people such as Mark and his friends. The kinds of 'distraction' fostered by the Internet, as Carr himself acknowledges, have become not just socially indispensable but professionally vital: 'the faster we're able to navigate [electronic] media and ... shift our attention among online tasks, the more valuable we're likely to become as employees and even as friends and colleagues' (140). Mark and his peers operate at this level of speed and dispersed attention because, for young people of their ilk, their futures depend on it. In Mark's case, one can go further still: it is a future he is helping build for himself, in his own image.

The relentless and unreflective drive towards this realization is further reinforced by Trent Reznor and Atticus Ross's electronic score, whose synthesized pulses, scratches and bleeps further inscribe digital textures and pace into the film text. Samuel Chase (2020) notes how frequently the film makes use of a rhythmic 'four-on-the-floor' beat associated with club music; the first cue in the hacking sequence, 'In Motion', being the key example, as the bus carrying the girls pulls in alongside the Phoenix house to the accompaniment of a 125 BPM bassline. Obviously, this is at some level appropriate to the contexts of the scene, though Chase's broader observation is that the music works *ambiguously* in relation to the action, as the pulsing beat is out of sync with the decelerated shots of the Phoenix party itself. The rhythm and rapid electronic note sequences are more matched to the actions of *Mark*, his hands fluttering across the keyboard, triggering quick movements of the windows on the computer screen – allied to, of course, the rapid, staccato patter of Mark's voiceover. As Chase adds, both here and via the subsequent cue ('A Familiar Taste'), while viewers are visually witnessing Mark's digital possession of female bodies and the dubious impacts of Facemash, they still get the driving, euphoric score: the music therefore might offset recognition of what Mark is actually doing, in terms of its ethical and misogynist implications (2020: 174–5).

Such techniques across the extent of the soundtrack underscore this chapter's broader point that the 'intensified' and 'accelerated' aspects of the film's aesthetics are never merely celebratory or unquestioned, or simply used (to refer back to Shaviro's terms) to manipulate the audience into a state of unreflective excitement. Rather, they become part of the film's problematic subject matter, a dimension of the very project whose creation the film seeks to narrate. By its own nature, this makes the film's stylistic approach ambivalent, perhaps disturbingly so, since it encourages a potentially excited response on the part of viewers, while also alluding to the questionable implications of what they are seeing. In terms of the score, Chase summarizes this approach as one of 'digital misempathy': the way in which the film's music purposely reinforces, through its elicitation of a response, anything Mark does to the benefit of Facebook's development, regardless of its impact on others or their feelings. Made up itself of digital elements, the score 'is always on the side of technology and money, and is disinterested in human sentiment. Almost any time the music displays or conveys emotion, it is with regards to the success of Facebook as a business' (2020: 171–2). As I have argued here, in fact, such strategies of 'misempathy', allied to the film's digital realism, are embraced not just in the score, but by all audio-visual aspects of the film's style.

One final but significant reflection to make on this particular sequence is its indebtedness to the aesthetics and narrative logics of the music video. Such expectations are perhaps not surprising, given Fincher's background as a director of the short video form, but the more important point is how such associations and techniques might be understood within the terms of *The Social Network*'s narrative and its representation of youth. Once again, we find that stylistic interventions on the film's part are never mere markers or superficial aspects of a youth-oriented contemporary style (the notional but not always clearly defined 'MTV aesthetic' sometimes associated with Hollywood from the mid-1980s onwards (Wyatt 1994)). Rather, such aesthetics are indivisible from what the film wants to represent in narrative terms: here, in particular, the film's appeal to 'virtual' realities and subjective viewpoints.

As Carol Vernallis has shown, one of the distinctive features of music video's short form is its tendency towards 'discontinuity', wherein the 'gaps' between images, most often stabilized and explained in narrative film by continuity editing techniques, are left unfilled and unresolved (2004: 37). Vernallis offers here a similar argument, applied in this case to the short form, to the one Shaviro makes for contemporary Hollywood feature filmmaking more broadly. Typically, rather than offering anything so clear as narrative continuity or dramatically fleshed-out scenes, the music video provides a series of images, the rhythm and logic of which are often dictated by the length of a musical phrase within the track. Alternatively, a music video might make use of the sequence of shots not so much to tell a story, at least in the classical sense, but to *hint* at a narrative through a sequence or juxtaposition of shots whose meaning is pieced together, either in relation to the lyrics of the song, or through the images' associations (38–44). What emerges overall out of this discussion is that the music video is at once a film that is not quite 'a film', at least as far as most common expectations of narrative cinema are concerned. It is, above all, a compact and essentially *atmospheric* and *affective* combination of images and sound, providing an often intense experience, though not necessarily one that evokes or mimetically represents actual characters in a clearly delineated diegetic world.

Nothing in *The Social Network* reaches this point of discontinuity; yet the ambiguities within the longer Facemash sequence allow, as noted earlier, for the depiction of a more subjectively oriented space and time. One further way the sequence does this, drawing here more specifically on the aesthetics of music video, is in its emphasis on graphic matches: a technique in which an aspect of composition, in the form either of a specific image detail or an object, recurs across two or more consecutive shots. As Vernallis notes, these sort of techniques, while sometimes used to join scenes, are seldom used in feature films because they are 'strikingly formal', serving to 'draw attention to [a film's] materials and production methods', and disrupting in the process the realist narrative aims of classical continuity style (Vernallis 2004: 30). In mostly non-narrative and expressive forms such as music video, by contrast, where the materiality of the image is more pronounced, such techniques are more frequent (ibid.). What graphic matches actually *mean* is, again, less important than their particular impact and display. Indeed, Vernallis's subsequent point is that the extended use of graphic matches serves as a form of 'visual rhyme' that is more musical than narrative in its use: images that 'carr[y] a chime of recognition and ... a momentary sense of completion' that are perhaps more striking for their ambiguity than what they might actually mean (ibid.).

The sequence from *The Social Network*, then, at one point cuts from the close-up of a pill, most likely Ecstasy, being placed on a girl's tongue (Figure 2.4), to a subsequent match shot of Mark taking a chug of beer (Figure 2.5); or then, from a shot of Dustin pouring vodka and orange juice into a plastic cup, to the same actions performed by a Phoenix Club bartender. Shortly afterwards, a shot of the Phoenix DJ tapping on his laptop segues into a shot of Mark's fingers moving swiftly over his own keyboard. Evidently, and as is usually the case with graphic matches, there is no obvious *causal* connection between the shots, in terms of how one action may impact on another; nor, as I have noted, is there any necessary assumption that these parallel actions in *The Social Network* are occurring simultaneously. The connections, it is implied, may exist only in Mark's mind, or indeed the

Figure 2.4 Graphic matches across space and time: the girls take a pill...

Figure 2.5 ... while Marks takes a chug of beer.

viewer's own, should they make that same imaginary link. Once more, the emphasis is on the fashioning of a personal, *virtual* space through digital interventions.

Acting Like a Child

The essentially self-contained, even solipsistic nature of this 'new media subject' – one that is connoted in terms of his or her mastery of digital technologies – also extends to the film's broader approaches to performance style. Both Bordwell (2011) and Schreiber (2016) have noted how the editing patterns in the film, partly because the relatively short shot lengths do not allow for sustained movement within the image, privilege the characters' faces above all else.[7] Bordwell highlights the fact that, as Mark, Jesse Eisenberg's immobility extends for most of the film even to his head and eyebrows, as it is frequently only his eyes that move at all. Schreiber adds that Mark's static manner becomes a stylistic principle, and most significantly, a motionless point of anchorage and control in the centre of the Facemash sequence, as indeed for most of the film (2016: 13).

Fincher, in his DVD commentary, has intriguingly referred to *The Social Network* as 'a movie about kids' faces', but what does this say about the 'kids' the film depicts? There is an important added sense here in which the fragmentary nature of the editing and the immobility that goes with it also undercut the possibility for expressivity. Shooting in more depth with minimally intrusive editing, or at least edits that allow for greater shot duration, naturally encourage a more sustained depiction of an actor's characterization within a given moment or scene. Such techniques bring screen performance closer to the conditions of theatrical acting, which more often requires the actor to represent the dramatic and emotional 'journey' of their character through extended periods of time, or allow one to observe details of performance, sometimes in relation to other characters on screen (Bordwell and Thompson 2004: 206; Baron and Carnicke 2008: 14). *The Social Network*'s screenplay, as its very opening scene testifies, contains its dramatic dynamics and peaks (and Sorkin, it is worth noting, has written frequently for the stage as well as for the screen); yet as we have seen, these are largely conveyed through the rhythmic back-and-forth movements of the editing in conjunction with the dialogue, denying the opportunities for more sustained performance dynamics.

There are a number of ways to make sense of this technique within the terms of both *The Social Network* and its situation within a wider field of contemporary youth culture and film. As Bordwell and Thompson have noted, like any element of a film's style, film acting makes the fullest sense in context, whether historical or generic (2004: 199–206). Acting styles, in other words, suit different films' form and story. This is not of course to say that film acting is a constant through all youth film traditions. In fact, *expressivity*, in terms of the actor using their whole body (and also costume) as a vehicle of character, and the types of sustained actor performance that highlights emotional transformation, are hallmarks of films such as *The Breakfast Club*, *Clueless* and *Easy A*. Similarly, in these films' ensemble set-ups, like those in *Superbad* or *Booksmart* (Wilde 2018), medium- or long-shot staging allows a better view of the dynamics of social interaction, one of youth film's main themes. *The Social Network*'s tactic, by contrast, is to resist these heightened individual or collective performance options. As Daniel Kasman (2010) has suggested in relation to a number of Fincher's films, as opposed to 'full-fledged, evolving scenes of melodrama', he offers us 'a montage-based cinema of this happened and then this happened and then this': a kind of informational aesthetic, focusing on the accumulation and processing of data. In the case of *The Social Network*, this is partly because these are characters that neither act nor react in such melodramatic terms, but move from action to action with a purposeful, businesslike logic.

Kent Jones pins down the film's editorial and narrative style as one in which 'time … is compressed, broken into mentally manageable units of work, work and more work'; adding that this has the effect, for the film's central protagonist, of 'cutting out the noise and distraction of other people and different viewpoints' (Jones 2010: 35). Social gatherings, along with their many joys and perils are simply less important to these characters, to the extent that these are rarely dramatized within the staging and cinematography. In some respects, this might seem to situate Mark on a different emotional and also creative level: Jones's observation that this is largely a film about *work* is a significant one. Yet it also underscores the monomania and intolerance of its main subject, stressing that he simply *has no time* for the types of evolving personal trajectories and emotional rollercoasters that are the hallmarks of other (youth) films. In this film, 'there is no time to linger … because there are always more satisfactions to be had' (ibid.).

But this technique in *The Social Network* also cuts both ways, since it means the protagonists are inadequately equipped, in reactive and expressive terms, to deal with the things that are eventually thrown at them, which can suddenly lay their youthfulness bare and exposed. As Bordwell notes (2011), the restrictions to facial movements in the film render aspects of the characters' performances open and enigmatic, with the most overtly emotional confrontations – Bordwell highlights a number of confrontations between Mark and Eduardo throughout the film – limited to small nuances of eye and mouth movement, and the use of eyeline matches as modes of accusation and response. Fincher's references to 'kids' faces' make sense here in terms of immaturity and callowness that informs many of the film's interactions and responses. Look, for instance, at the way Jesse Eisenberg's response to his being dumped, at the end of the film's opening scene – conveyed, again, in a mere shift of the eyes and brows, and a slight narrowing of the lips – is to look vaguely confused, before he picks up, looks at and then puts down his glass of beer. Or note, in a different context, and as outlined by Bordwell (2011), how Andrew Garfield expresses his betrayal in the Facebook offices not via 'bug-eyed surprise or frowning bafflement', but merely through a look of 'dazed, slightly perplexed surprise'. In fact, in this same scene, Eisenberg's facial response does not indicate any sense of revenge or smarminess. Instead, he offers the same puzzled, somewhat confused look he gives in the Thirsty Scholar scene, looking for all the world as though Eduardo has stolen his lunch money rather than smashed his laptop (Figure 2.6). As Bordwell argues, such under-playing in narrative film works in tandem with the narrative context, which supplies the added information needed for interpretation. But in this specific context, I would add, it also stresses the visibility of immature thought processes and inexperience.

In one respect, such nuanced approaches to acting as those on display in *The Social Network* are striking, not because they are unrealistic (they are not), but because the types of responses in *The Social Network* are at odds with the kinds of emotive, gestural short-hands

Figure 2.6 'A movie about kids' faces'.

(the 'playing of emotion', in other words) that are part of a familiar yet *un*realistic typology of screen acting (Gladwell 2019: 145–67). A cumulative effect of this technique in *The Social Network* is to render the expressive and emotional range of its characters strangely muted and *inarticulate*, out of sync with the verbal and technological virtuosity they otherwise exhibit throughout the film. This is in one respect a means of registering the distance between the protagonists' more flippant actions, above all Mark's, and their drastic consequences. But the sense of emotional inarticulacy is entirely adequate to the drama it depicts, precisely because it reiterates and reminds us that these are still *just kids*; kids, in effect, playing at being something else for which, developmentally, they are minimally equipped.

The Cultural Moment: Film History and Irony

As this study has so far explored, *The Social Network* takes an ambivalent approach to a subject that is, itself, uncertainly and dramatically positioned between different worlds: between Harvard's frosty sanctum and the sun-soaked brashness of Palo Alto; between the irresponsibility of youth and the demands, both economic and ethical, of creating Facebook; between the exhilaration of speed and the hollowness at the centre of the whirlwind. In this final section of the chapter, I look more closely at *The Social Network*'s ambiguous and sometimes ironic relationship to cinematic culture more specifically; and in particular, how Fincher and Sorkin's film plays with one further dichotomy, in terms of the competing registers of 'high' and 'low' cultural reference.

I have given attention to the relevance of *The Social Network* within Sorkin's wider body of work, but in this instance, it is useful to look at the film in relation to some of Fincher's other movies. As I have discussed elsewhere with reference to *Gone Girl* (2014), Fincher's work frequently walks a self-aware line between high-cultural contexts and those of 'trash' (Archer 2017). In *Gone Girl*, for instance, the film (like the 2012 Gillian Flynn novel on which it is based) employs modernist techniques of multiple, unreliable narrators and a complex flashback structure. In this respect, it adheres to many of the hallmarks of the so-called 'puzzle plot' film; a mode in turn-of-the-century Hollywood cinema that gestures to the genre literacy of its audience, offering them more challenging narrative ploys (Bordwell 2006; Buckland 2009). At the same time, *Gone Girl* also embraces the aesthetics of 'mass' or 'low' culture as part of its fabric: its thriller plot, for instance, exploits knowledge and plotting drawn from true-crime books and TV cop shows, and melodramatic tropes from abduction- or stalker movies (Archer 2017).

As *Gone Girl* exemplifies, Fincher's career has to a large extent been defined by this capacity to bring production-value sheen, high-cultural references and auteurist touches to otherwise 'generic' material.[8] His breakthrough feature film, *Se7en* (1995), took the serial-killer form and embellished it with a plethora of mythical and literary allusions, from the Bible to Dante's *Inferno* to Chaucer's *Canterbury Tales* – without, it should be noted, going much further into these texts than Brad Pitt's Detective Mills does, frantically glossing them via his Cliffs Notes primers. Indeed, Mills' older colleague, Somerset (Morgan Freeman), describes the city library to which he retreats as somewhere 'far away from here': this is a world and a time in which no one, it seems, actually reads anymore. Later films such as *Zodiac* (2007) and *The Girl with the Dragon Tattoo* (2011) made similar use of literary or scholarly allusions, with their references to Old Testament scripture and the mysteries of cryptography. As with *Se7en* and *Gone Girl*, these films also draw on complex narrational techniques, though always within the otherwise 'pulpy' cinematic trappings of genre film: the police procedural in *Zodiac*; the 'closed-room' mystery and (again) the serial-killer film in *The Girl with the Dragon Tattoo* (Archer 2013: 11–12).

Such surface allusions to older media forms, and the veering between high and low culture, is in many respects the texture of the world Fincher's films describe, and has its origins in the adverts and music videos Fincher made at the start of his career (Browning 2010: 1–22). Fincher's *Express Yourself* promo for Madonna (1989), for instance, a lavishly expensive production for the time, drew significantly on imagery from Fritz Lang's classic film *Metropolis* (1927); a distinctive example of the way music video often tends to lift and 'repurpose' wider cultural allusions within its short-form span. This same approach often finds its way into Fincher's feature films: we might note, for example, how in *The Girl with the Dragon Tattoo* Fincher occasionally shoots Rooney Mara's Lisbeth Salander with specific allusions to the actor Renée Falconetti, echoing her performance as the title character in Carl Dreyer's *The Passion of Joan of Arc* (1928).

These remain mostly fleeting visual allusions within their new location, and as such, they might arguably operate as forms of pastiche; a part even of the work's aesthetic texture, a form of decoration, rather than the subject of a sustained dialogue with the original work. Jim Collins (2002) has discussed such aesthetics in terms of 'high-pop': a style marked by the appropriation of high-cultural motifs and markers within the commodified world of mass entertainment. For Deborah

Cartmell and Imelda Whelehan, high-pop is characterized by its in-difference to erstwhile oppositional culture, embracing as it does high-cultural allusion within the same contexts as pop-culture consumerism (2010: 52–4). What happens in this process is that any idea of different or competing cultural value is effectively flattened: high art and trash are simply part of the same text, interwoven and inseparable. In terms of the protagonists of *The Social Network*, there is the related sense that this flattening extends to the broader notions of culture, con-sumption and value the film explores, with a particular emphasis on the levelling of culture itself in the Internet age: an age in which, merely to use the examples highlighted in the film, students' 'hotness' and the value of various European artworks (as per Mark's art-history class, where he elicits comments from Facebook users for his assignments) can equally be rated online, reduced to data and statistical evaluation.

As noted earlier, the film's Facemash sequence leaves interpretation and its veracity open to question. But it is perhaps too easy to overlook the way that *The Social Network* plays with its *own* sense of factual record more generally. The decision to structure the film around its two deposition scenes – something we only discern fifteen minutes into the film, after both the scene in The Thirsty Scholar and the invention of Facemash – in effect renders everything we otherwise see and hear the product not only of flashback, but of reported speech, and there-fore subject to contestation (indeed, Mark's first line in the filmic 'present' of the deposition scene is 'That's not what happened'). Harris (2010) is not alone amongst commentators in spotting the structural allusion here to *Rashomon* (1950), the celebrated Akira Kurosawa film that views the same crime (a rape and murder) from multiple and in-compatible perspectives, and which remains a pre-eminent forerunner of the more recent puzzle-plot film. The fact that this is somewhat played down as a narrative technique in *The Social Network* (it is only in this first scene, for example, that the truth of the testimony is really questioned), and the fact that a viewer might consequently see the film as a more verbatim depiction of events, only reinforces Sheehan's point (2013: 42) that the truth gets lost amidst the story that gets told, and then *re*-told. In any case, as the very nature of the depositions reminds us, the contested story in *The Social Network*, in an era of mass communications, does not rely purely on hearsay or subjective interpretation: there are a plethora of emails, blog posts and con-tractual data to at least substantiate the litigants' claims. Perhaps more to the point, the film wears its allusions to *Rashomon* lightly because, in the end, the narrative of *The Social Network* reduces down to a tussle over money and intellectual property, *not* the uncertainty of evidence or the problem of subjectivity, which are the main themes of Kurosawa's film. There is no time for philosophy in the accelerated world of Facebook's creation – nor, for that matter, reflections on Japanese art cinema.

This form of *unreflective* allusion to high-cultural cinematic texts also informs *The Social Network*'s structural and referential debt to Orson Welles and Herman Mankiewicz's *Citizen Kane* (1941).[9] The ending of Sorkin and Fincher's film offers an image of empire-building as spiritual and emotional isolation, with Mark, one of the world's richest men, alone in a lawyer's elevated office, striving and failing to make contact – via Facebook, naturally – with Erica. This is an image not remote from that of Charles Foster Kane seen in Xanadu, the palatial residence that houses Welles' reclusive and lonely media magnate, at once the most materially wealthy and spiritually bankrupt man in America. But the further ironic 'repurposing' of *Citizen Kane* in *The Social Network* relates to the latter film's specific subject matter, and the origin of Mark's particular empire. In the earlier film, Charles Foster Kane takes up a role as owner of the New York *Inquirer*, a small newspaper for which he has grand ambitions. In one of the film's early scenes, a late-night session in Kane's editorial office ends with him writing out his 'Declaration of Principles', to be printed on the front page of the morning edition: a pledge to the *Inquirer*'s readers that it 'will "tell all the news honestly" and be "a fighting and tireless champion of the people"' (Ehrlich 2006: 69).

The scene in *Citizen Kane*, which shows Kane writing his declaration against a window, is echoed in a compositionally very similar shot in *The Social Network*, when Eduardo writes his hotness comparison algorithm with a marker pen on the dorm room window (Figure 2.7).

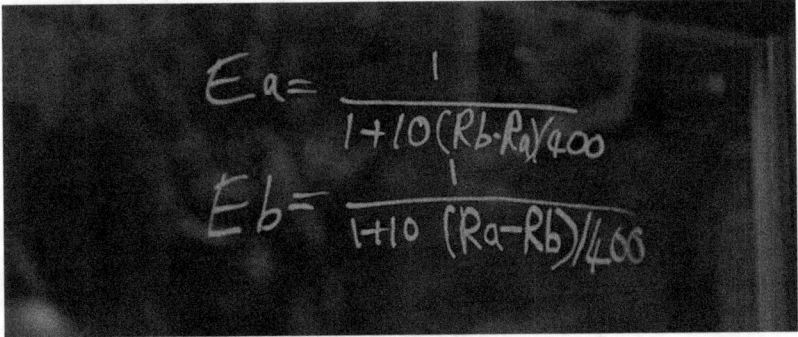

Figure 2.7 The Facemash algorithm, ironically framed.

Here, we see the scene via a shot through the window itself, as Eduardo and Mark describe the algorithm's function:

EDUARDO: Give each girl a base rating of 1400. At any given time, 'Girl A' has a rating R-a and 'Girl B' has a rating R-b.

MARK: When any two girls are matched up there's an expectation of which will win based on their current rating, right?

EDUARDO: (tapping the window) Yes. And those expectations are expressed this way.

MARK: Let's write it.

The visual similarities to the scene from *Citizen Kane* are significant here mainly in terms of the disjunctions between what each scene narrates: a declaration of journalistic commitment, on the one hand; and on the other, an algorithm used intrusively to compare the sexual attractiveness of unsuspecting students. To underscore both the ironic juxtapositions at work in the scene, as well as its narrative implications – the scene is a reminder that the algorithm which at some level launched Facebook was *Eduardo*'s not Mark's – the camera closes in on the equation from inside the room, its mathematical complexity giving it a gravitas as if looking at Newton's law of gravity or $E = mc^2$ (it is worth noting that the sequence also has a visual precedent in *A Beautiful Mind* [Howard 2001], the biopic of mathematician John Nash, who writes his equations on the windows at Princeton). It is once more typical of *The Social Network*'s ambiguities that, in foregrounding the historical significance of this moment, it reminds us in this same instance of what aims the equation will be in service.

This is a key instance of what I would call *The Social Network*'s technique of double address, in which two very distinct cultural contexts play off each other in tension. Fincher has referred to *The Social Network* as 'the *Citizen Kane* of John Hughes movies' (quoted in Harris 2010); possibly a jokey remark, but one that also raises the significance of what such reference points really mean in the specific contexts of youth cinema. This question of literary or other cultural allusion in wider films about youth, in films ranging from *Clueless* to *Cruel Intentions* (Kumble 1999), to *O* (Nelson 2001) and to *Easy A*, has engaged numerous scholars. Some, for example, have focused on the significance of classic literary fiction or drama as a form of 'hypertext' or 'palimpsest' that engages reflectively with the source material (as Kaklamanidou argues regarding *Easy A* (2018: 35–7)), or have viewed adaptation across context as a playful reflection on changing mores, values and cultural competences (as Esther Sonnet (1999) argues in her discussion of *Clueless*). Despite its visual and structural indebtedness to *Citizen Kane*, which itself employs a similar flashback structure to Fincher and Sorkin's film, it would be a stretch to consider *The Social Network* as an 'adaptation', in comparison with the way *Easy A* and *Clueless* foreground their indebtedness to Nathaniel Hawthorne's *The Scarlett Letter* and Jane Austen's *Emma*, respectively. Yet *The Social Network* is no less engaged in a similar dialogue around the changing conditions of 'classic' narratives in an American, millennial context.

A key difference here, though, is the less tangible nature of the allusion, which remains more of a trace, an acknowledgement that viewers *might* identify, but one which is hardly obvious. As Kaklamanidou notes, classic novels or works by Shakespeare do not merely provide widely recognized, structurally universal and copyright-exempt dramatic content. Such texts are also 'embedded in the American educational system' (2018: 34), to the extent that they are *already* part of the experience of American cultural life. *Citizen Kane*, by contrast, as much as it might be a staple of the film studies- and film-critical canon, does not enjoy the same kind of familiarity or universality, especially since its more experimental form guards against this possibility. Indeed, the deliberately obscure allusions to the film in *The Social Network* echo this sense of the earlier film's lesser prominence within popular culture, and especially in the life of the young. Importantly, none of the protagonists in *The Social Network* recognize that they are visually quoting a scene from *Citizen Kane*, or even *A Beautiful Mind*. But this is precisely the point since it allows a viewer that *does* acknowledge the allusion to assess it in terms of the similarities and discrepancies between the two films, and how the later film plays off the earlier one. As its allusions to Welles and Mankiewicz's film appear to suggest, *The Social Network* narrates a similarly profound shift in American media and communications and is in turn a story worthy of comparison. The comparison mostly ends there, though – and it is notable that, in this instance, *Citizen Kane* and the history and ideas sketched in it might be of little interest to the subjects of *The Social Network*. As we are led to believe, in fact, the core Facebook team were more enamoured of epics like *Troy* (Petersen 2004), or of Tom Cruise movies such as *Top Gun* (Scott 1986), even going so far as to name two of its early servers 'Maverick' and 'Iceman' in honour of the latter film (Kirkpatrick 2010a: 56–57, 97).[10]

Culture 2.0

The aim of this chapter has been to highlight the ambivalent way *The Social Network* employs the audio-visual forms of contemporary popular film. The film embraces many of the conventions of 'intensified continuity' style, especially in its emphasis on the intensities of speed, be this in the editing, its dialogue or its musical soundtrack, or in its focus on the new digital spaces of much twenty-first-century experience. I have shown how the film purposefully engages with the potential shallowness of such aesthetics, in such a way even as to expose its characters' lack of 'depth' or maturity.

My final reflections above are intended, furthermore, to emphasize *The Social Network*'s complex situation within cinematic culture: a film that purposefully places itself alongside *Citizen Kane* while also calling into ironic question its equivalences. Such allusions further highlight the ambiguities in the film that this chapter has been working to elucidate. The allusion here becomes ironic, shallow; yet at the same time, the *narrative* similarities still persist in some form. Like *The Social Network*, *Citizen Kane* is ultimately a story of youthful enthusiasm corrupted by wealth and power, resulting in the abandonment of values and the isolation of its billionaire subject. And like *Citizen Kane*, *The Social Network* also delivers a portrait of American energy and – in the eyes of its young protagonists, at least – *idealism*, whatever we ourselves might choose to make of these ideals.

It is this hesitation on the part of the film between different cultural and aesthetic contexts that underscores the uncertain and complex situation of the very subject it describes. *The Social Network*, in stylistic terms, exploits many of the trappings of a popular contemporary aesthetic seen often as targeting a youth audience; while at the same time, using these same aesthetics to cast a more ambivalent eye over its story of youth. In a very specific way, though, this uncertain situation of *The Social Network* is apt for narrating the birth of a company *itself* positioned at an intersection between different, even apparently opposing cultural spheres.

It is important to stress that, from the perspective of those driving it, Facebook represented not just a lucrative invention for the social media age, but a defining cultural moment. Matt Cohler, who helped lead Facebook's product management team in its early years, went so far as to describe the 'unique creative zeitgeist' of which Facebook was the centre, comparing it to 'jazz in New York in the 1940s or punk in the 1970s, or the first Viennese school of the late eighteenth century' (Kirkpatrick 2010a: 152).

It is a similar attitude that *The Social Network* strives to capture. When Mark, in the scene quoted earlier, says *Let's write it*, he does so with the immediacy and inspired energy of youth, and more specifically of *creative* youth. It is also, as Mark states, a work of *writing*. No one ever reads in *The Social Network,* or puts pen to paper, or picks up a paintbrush. These young people work and create *in code,* and what they produce – visually and imaginatively, not merely functionally – matters to them.[11] Whether or not one shares their view, to these protagonists, it *is* a 'unique creative zeitgeist' they see themselves as creating. And they have a lot of 'friends' who would agree.

Of course, such allusions to artistic innovation, and especially a spirit of *counter-culture,* to pick up on Cohler's chosen example of jazz and punk, beg a fundamental question. For all its possibilities as a communicative and expressive tool, or as a work of website design and function, Facebook, as *The Social Network* reminds us by its conclusion, is also a billion-dollar *business.* For all the grander claims of those helping to shape the Facebook world, how does one square Facebook's cultural self-perceptions both with its commercial realities and its rise towards a form of global domination? As the following chapter explores, these contradictions form an important part of *The Social Network*'s narrative design.

Notes

1 Readers might wish to perform a Google search of this question (a question usually ascribed to the film, rather than any other source) to see some answers. Most point out the obvious fact that, for Mark's statement to be true, an unlikely one in four Chinese would need to have genius IQs.

2 For a summary of the significance of the sequence shot as a counter-aesthetic to intensified continuity style, see Archer (2016).

3 The film's opening lines offer in some regards a classic example of what Nobel laureate Daniel Kahnemann, in his book *Thinking, Fast and Slow,* describes as 'System 1' thinking: one that, in contrast to System 2's 'effortful mental activities [and] computations', 'operates automatically and quickly, with little or no effort' (2011: 20–1). It is in the less difficult and therefore more common System 1 mode that people make intuitive snap judgements, often based on a superficial or impressionistic assessment of data.

4 The 180° rule is the principle, central to classical continuity style and its respect for spatial legibility, that any given exchange in a scene should be filmed behind an imaginary 180° line, beyond which the camera should not move. In the opening scene, the camera set-ups never transgress this line.

5 *The Social Network* was filmed with Red One MX digital cameras, and cut using the Adobe Premiere Editing System.

6 Brand is the film's semi-fictionalized version of the 29-year-old Harvard graduate Paul Podesta. Brand is played by the (at the time) slightly younger Jonah Hill.

7 As Bordwell identifies in his analysis of intensified continuity (2006: 121–38), the close-up is the natural shot choice within a system favouring decreased shot lengths.

8 Or perhaps more accurately, since Fincher does not write his own scripts, he has an eye for screenplays that permit him to do this.

9 Fincher's father, Jack, had written an unfilmed screenplay about Mankiewicz's contributions to *Citizen Kane* before his death in 2003; the screenplay was finally filmed by Fincher as *Mank* (2020).

10 Allegedly, Zuckerberg, a competitive fencer and also a fluent reader of ancient Greek, had a penchant for quoting Brad Pitt's lines as Achilles from *Troy* – in one instance, following a call from lawyers during the Winklevoss/Narendra lawsuit (Kirkpatrick 2010a: 97).

11 On the aesthetics of coding and its relationship to traditional ideas of the literary, see Vishal Chandra's *Geek Sublime* (2013). Steve Jobs famously spoke of his work at Apple as operating 'at the intersection of technology and liberal arts' (Isaacson 2011: 494), a point developed throughout Walter Isaacson's biography of Jobs.

3 'I'm CEO, Bitch': The Conundrum of Capital

When pared down, *The Social Network* operates dramatically around the reconcilability – or otherwise – of commerce and cool. Through Mark and Eduardo's evolving and unfolding relationship, the film asks how the practicalities of operating a business are squared with its notional ethos and aims. Sorkin's dialogue encapsulates this dilemma roughly halfway through the film, shortly after Facebook has taken off on the Harvard campus:

EDUARDO: ... it's time to monetize the site.

MARK: What does that mean?

EDUARDO: It means it's time for the website to generate revenue.

MARK: No, I know what the word means. I'm asking how do you want to do it?

EDUARDO: Advertising.

MARK: No.

EDUARDO: We've got 4000 members.

MARK: Cause Facebook is cool. If we start installing pop-ups for Mountain Dew it's not gonna –

EDUARDO: Well I wasn't thinking Mountain Dew but at some point – and I'm talking as the business end of the company – the site –

MARK: We don't even know what it is yet. We don't know what it is, we don't know what it can be, we don't know what it will be. We know that it's cool: that is a priceless asset I'm not giving it up.

This same conversation is taken up again shortly afterwards when Mark and Eduardo meet up with Sean in New York:

EDUARDO: Settle an argument for us, would you? I say it's time to

DOI: 10.4324/9781003161936-4

	start making money from Facebook but Mark doesn't want advertising. Who's right?
SEAN:	Neither of you yet. Facebook is cool, that's what it's got going for it.
MARK:	Yeah.
SEAN:	You don't want to ruin it with ads because ads aren't cool.
MARK:	Exactly.
SEAN:	It's like you're throwing the greatest party on campus and someone's telling you it's gotta be over at 11:00.
MARK:	That's exactly right.
SEAN:	You don't even know what the thing is yet.
MARK:	I said exactly that.

Neither Sean nor Mark can offer any real explanation as to what makes Facebook 'cool'. What *is* clear, however, is what cool is *not* – which in this case is any indication on Facebook's part that it is actively trying to make money. 'Ads aren't cool': to sell stuff via the site would be, as Sean suggests, to spoil the party. Yet as Eduardo points out in the cab after the New York meeting, 'I'm trying to pay for the party'. Mark's response, echoing Sean's, is not so much a coherent answer, as a statement of the impasse at which Mark and Eduardo now find themselves, 'There won't be a party unless it's cool'. And so it goes around. Yet of course, hanging over this exchange is Sean's ultimate assessment of Facebook's potential value, related by Eduardo at his deposition:

SEAN:	This is no time to take your chips down. A million dollars isn't cool. You know what's cool?
EDUARDO:	A *billion* dollars ... And that shut everybody up.
SEAN:	And that's where you're headed.

As I argue in this chapter, one of the achievements of *The Social Network* is its anatomization of cool in the film's early twenty-first-century contexts. This matters for the study of cinematic youth cultures because, as *The Social Network* reiterates, cool in the era of Web 2.0 is dominated and defined by *People* 2.0 – in other words, the young, and even more specifically, the young, media-savvy and technologically connected. Distinctive to these specific contexts is the way that, in the social media-dominated era, the trappings of youthful rebellion that have sometimes driven ideas of cool, often in response to capitalist culture, here also drive capitalism itself. As Sean reiterates, ads aren't cool, but making a billion dollars definitely *is*. Being cool and making money, if the latter means trying to sell stuff, are irreconcilable aims. But cool in itself also sells. How so, and why at this particular time and place? *The Social Network* works through these questions and these contradictions.

And the Geek Shall Inherit the Earth: Capitalism and the Appropriation of Cool

At the end of *The Social Network*, assistant lawyer Marylin offers a concluding view of the film's main protagonist: 'You're not an asshole, Mark. You're just trying so hard to be'. In Chapter 1, I highlighted the extent to which Mark and his peers are social outsiders (in terms of their geekiness, their Jewishness), while reiterating that this exclusion operates within the already elite contexts of being white males in a Harvard University environment. Marylin's pithy but generous assessment may be too forgiving of Mark. But it also serves to remind him of the vast privilege underpinning his behaviour since Marylin hints here at the *performance* of disaffection and disrespect, on the part of boys with no intrinsic need or aptitude to play such roles. Why try to be an asshole in the first place?

Returning briefly to the discussion of Jewishness, Mark's behaviour and manner arguably situate him within a broader history and discourse around Jewish masculinity and agency. In particular, Mark embodies certain aspects of the 'tough Jew'; a later twentieth-century identity, as Nathan Abrams has discussed, seen as a response to (self-) perceptions of Jewish passivity and weakness (Abrams 2012: 91–133). Such an idea is incorporated literally into the text of films such as *Knocked Up* (2007), in which *schlubby* Jewish stoners, incarnated here by Seth Rogen and Jonah Hill, can rhapsodize about Steven Spielberg's film *Munich* (2005) because it features Jews 'cappin' motherfuckers' (110). Looking though at broader cinematic contexts, *The Social Network* can also be viewed within the longer representational traditions of American youth and the centrality of rebellion within it. Both Shary (2005) and Driscoll (2011), for instance, highlight the importance to youth film of the 'JD' figure: the 'juvenile delinquent', incarnated in a range of films from the 1950s, and given most iconic form by an actual 'J.D.', James Dean, in *Rebel Without a Cause* (Ray 1955). The latter film may be nearly seventy years old, but Dean's embodiment of teenage disaffection is important for our understanding of recent youth cinema in two ways.[1] Firstly, his portrayal of Jim Stark in *Rebel Without a Cause* is specifically one of 'upwardly-

mobile middle-class' malaise (Shary 2005: 22), during a period of unprecedented consumerist affluence in American life. From this perspective, Stark's (self-)destructive behaviours seem to derive not so
much from social disenfranchisement, as from the *anomie* born out of
suburban middle-class prosperity. Secondly, James Dean's cinematic
iconicity as this cause-less 'rebel', and the coincidental link between his
own initials and the juvenile delinquent figure, mean that in later cinematic contexts – especially the 'post-modern' phase of the youth film
in the later 1980s and 1990s – the JD figure fuses with the iconography
of James Dean, stripped of any residual socio-political meaning and
returned as pure image or cliché (Driscoll 2011: 57). This is seen,
perhaps unironically, in the form of *The Breakfast Club*'s John Bender
(Judd Nelson); but more self-consciously, in the form of Christian
Slater's 'J.D.' (his actual character name is Jason Dean), the privileged
'bad boy' in *Heathers* (Lehmann 1989).

In some respects, the title character of *Ferris Bueller's Day Off* offers
another important revision of this same figure within an age shaped by
consumerism and image culture. The shift from J.D. to F.B. might on
the surface seem unlikely, but the film's plot is, after all, one long
celebration of truancy. The difference here, as with J.D. in *Heathers*, is
the nature of the young protagonist's 'angst'. I already noted in a
previous chapter how Ferris cares more about not having a car than
about European socialism; and as a number of writers on youth film
identify, Ferris Bueller embodies a drift in the politics of the 1980s
away from broader counter-cultural consciousness, and even from the
sex-and-drugs-oriented rebellions of prior decades, towards a 'politics
[of] consumption' (Shary 2005: 54; see also Driscoll 2011; Lewis 1992).
In the same way that Mark in *The Social Network* wears his Adidas
slides as a form of signature, Matthew Broderick's character sports a
beret for part of the film; a gesture whose nod to Che Guevara-type
radicalism is offset by the fact that Ferris, while wearing the beret, is
also riding in the Ferrari he so desperately covets. The beret in effect
underscores Ferris's ironic and hedonistic appropriation of radical
chic. Less concerned with changing society at a structural level, his aim
is to show his friends the best time. He encourages both his peers and
the audience to embrace life's material and experiential benefits; providing, that is, they already possess the sufficient means – a top-range
computer, a friend with a Ferrari, and a generous weekly allowance –
in order to do so.

Clueless is also a significant point of discussion here, in terms of the
permeation of Black American slang and culture (especially Coolio's
1995 track 'Rollin' With My Homies') into the updated social fabric of

Rebel Without a Cause: the affluent, upper-middle-class West Coast (Driscoll 2011: 58).[2] In striving to work out why privileged white American youth should appropriate Black American rap and hip-hop, Jim McGuigan identifies a historical association of cool with an attitude or 'pose' adopted by the cultures of the dispossessed. Many black Americans, for example, their culture and attitudes shaped both by inherited African warrior traditions, and by the historical scars of slavery, adopted a form of resistance to the dictates of modern American society conveyed above all else by personal style (McGuigan 2009: 3). In many of its twentieth-century manifestations on either side of the Atlantic, via numerous subcultures, cool manifested a kind of detachment, often hedonistic or disdainful, from the dominant culture and lifestyle.

Out of these contexts, of course, such a pose can seem superficial. As Driscoll notes, *Clueless* has been criticized for its tendency to smooth out any trace of the racial divisions and tensions that West Coast 'gangsta rap' of the period evoked, and which were more concretely manifest in the Los Angeles riots of 1992.[3] The fact that *Clueless* does *not* highlight this disjuncture is, I would argue in response, part of its broader ironic point, which is that even a form as violent and disenfranchised as gangsta rap can still be commodified as another mode of subcultural identification for middle-class whites. For McGuigan, the intriguing property of rap is that a genre often seen initially as hostile towards a mainstream white audience, an audience notionally excluded from its inclusive frames of reference or address, should be embraced so enthusiastically by this same white audience – either in spite of, or maybe *because* of, its 'brutal, misogynistic and homophobic features' (McGuigan 2009: 98). But in this same appropriation by the middle-class white mainstream, the socio-economic and political contexts underpinning much rap – those, say, of police victimization and under-privilege – may also be lost in the process of cultural translation. To borrow the title of 50 Cent's 2003 album and subsequent 2005 film, there exist contexts in which to *Get Rich or Die Tryin'* is effectively a statement of intent, rather than simply the fashionable or ironic pose it might be to the same artist's affluent white fans.

Mark's own somewhat tepid affectation of insolent urban cool in *The Social Network* suggests an intention to align with the trappings of a disaffected style, without having to worry about the actual circumstances or contexts informing the culture from which such style emerged. The film's focus on the physical trappings of this commodified 'dissent', especially in the form of Mark's clothes, is appropriate

Figure 3.1 Mark's 'fuck-you flip-flops' (plus socks).

in its attention to *surface*. His socks aside, Mark's incongruous tendency to wear his slides in all weathers, even in the Cambridge winter, is just one way this attitude of dissenting difference is underlined (Figure 3.1).[4] Even in Palo Alto, where the climate is more suited to Mark's footwear, the insistence on the shorts, slides and tee-shirt combo nods to a specific historical aspect of Silicon Valley style, in which the calculated refusal to wear anything resembling office attire serves as a badge of anti-corporate intent.

Within the peer-influence of an increasingly youthful Silicon Valley, allegiance to such (anti-)dress codes – what Steven Levy describes as the self-styled 'geek proletariat' look (Levy 2020: 1)[5] – could also be instrumental in getting hired: Adam Fisher's history of the Valley recounts, for example, how interviewees at Google during its earliest years were told to 'go home and change' if they were naive enough to turn up in a suit (Fisher 2018: 280). In like fashion, the casual look Mark essays even in the lawsuit hearings, especially when compared to the formal attire of Cameron, Tyler and Eduardo, mark his mental separation from, and contempt for, the formalities of the proceedings, in the same way that his clothing elsewhere shows his possibly feigned disregard for the inclemency of Cambridge's winter weather. It is also clear, by the film's concluding scenes, that this stylistic pose has been appropriated both as an *attitude*, and a shared understanding with Sean, that fatefully excludes Eduardo:

SEAN: You think we were gonna let you parade around in your ridiculous suits pretending you were running this company?

EDUARDO: (to Sean) Sorry, my Prada's at the cleaners (to Mark) along with my hoodie and my fuck-you flip-flops, you pretentious douchebag.

This scene, prior to the party celebrating Facebook's millionth member, brings to a conclusion the chain of events triggered by the New York meeting. Eduardo here calls into question Sean's and Mark's sartorial badges of rebellion, at the same moment that Sean, the Silicon Valley bad-boy, has pulled presidency of the company away from him: a company, moreover, that is about to get these 'bad' boys extremely rich (though *dyin' tryin'*, needless to say, was never here a realistic possibility).

Eduardo's reference to Mark's and Sean's combination of designer gear and 'fuck-you' streetwear is a telling one since it encapsulates the incorporation of attitude as a kind of upmarket style option, a nod to rebellion within the privileged terrain of high-end fashion.[6] *The Social Network*, though, has already by this point highlighted how deeply disconnected Facebook is from any real radicalism and counter-cultural position. At the interview for interns in one of Harvard's computer labs, five boys are hacking their way through various levels of encryption, knocking back shots every ten lines of code they write, as well as at designated intervals signalled by a bell. The sound mix here emphasizes the raucous crowd, drowning out Mark and Eduardo's conversation, creating a powerful impression of energy and excitement. When Mark finally announces the winners, shaking their hands with a clipped 'Welcome to Facebook', we see Dustin quickly snap on the chorus of the Dead Kennedy's 1979 track 'California Über Alles', as the watching crowd spills around a smiling Mark, with Eduardo watching on, entranced.

The track used in the film is probably not the actual one used at the interview – Mezrich, as well as Sorkin's original script, suggests that the track was Dr. Dre's 'California Love', in itself another indicator of how aspirational West Coast rap culture was to the young Facebook creatives (Mezrich 2010: 158). 'California Über Alles' is a brilliantly chosen alternative, however, and not just for the abrasive burst of guitar and vocals it provides. The song's appropriation of lines from the German national anthem, with its still lingering Nazi-era con-notations, is mapped on to its dystopian vision of California ruled over by New Age tyrants, with their determination to enforce compulsory jogging and put meditation on the school curriculum. And in the re-ference to the 'Zen fascists' that 'will control you', the song also taps into what was in the 1970s an emerging computer-industry culture of corporate and technological disruption, concealed within the trappings of Eastern spiritualism and West-Coast 'cool' (Fisher 2018: 17–73). But such ironies, *The Social Network* seems to suggest, are lost on the film's protagonists: the song's dissenting spirit, extracted from its contexts, becomes simply another pose; its use here merely one more indication of cool capitalism's contradictory energies.[7]

As McGuigan notes, cool has entered the lexicon of corporate capitalism as a mode of description and a working ethos, especially when the coolness invoked by corporations 'incorporates counter-cultural traditions and deploy[s] signs of "resistance"' (McGuigan 2009: 124). In *The Social Network*, as inspired by Sean, Mark eventually gets himself a set of business cards reading: 'I'm CEO, Bitch': in itself a perfect encapsulation of corporate power disavowed by the push of Mark's asshole attitude. Both Mark and Sean, in fact, embody the way in which Silicon Valley's attitude of dissent and disruption makes it a centre for technologically driven capitalism to flourish. The team working on what became the first Macintosh computer, for example, which appeared eventually in 1984, actually hoisted a skull and crossbones over their building to highlight that they were the 'renegade pirates' within Apple's otherwise bureaucratic set-up – even though, of course, they still worked for Apple (Fisher 2018: 108). The now legendary '1984' TV ad for the Macintosh used an image evoking George Orwell's 'Big Brother' as a veiled allegory for Apple's vision of the IBM-led computer industry, with the Macintosh personified as a heroic individual, coming to bring a figurative sledgehammer to this notionally controlling monopoly (Fisher 2018: 112–6; Isaacson 2011: 162–5).[8]

Under the stewardship of Steve Jobs as CEO, and then in tandem with designer Jony Ive, Apple established the idea of tech products – formerly impersonal, functional tools for work and business – as *cool*: from the original Macintosh, through to the candy-coloured iMacs of the 1990s, pinnacling with the unveiling in the 2000s of the iPod, iPhone and iPad. Jobs, together with advertising partner Lee Clow, devised a brand strategy in the late 1990s that would ally product design and function with the idea of radical cultural and political innovation. Apple's 'Think Different' campaign, in its TV version, edited together shots of iconic figures deemed to bridge the fields of philosophy, arts and politics – Gandhi, Bob Dylan, Martin Luther King, John Lennon – along with the words, 'Here's to the crazy ones, the misfits, the rebels, the troublemakers … [The ones] who push the human race forward' (Isaacson 2011: 329). This is the same attitude that, although slightly different in tone, permeated the attitude of

Facebook as a growing company. Following Ben Barry's 'Move Fast and Break Things' sign in 2008 (discussed in the previous chapter), later posters around the Facebook offices took a more obvious leaf from Apple's playbook, featuring images of 'fearless people, underdogs who risked things for selfless causes: Dolores Huerta, Shirley Chisholm, Cesar Chavez', all of them 'heroes of the downtrodden', and intriguing identification figures for Facebook's mostly white, male executives and six figure-salaried engineers (Levy 2020: 243).[9]

Other companies have shown a similar ability to integrate affirmative, even politicized messages into their marketing strategies through advertising; most obviously Nike, who in the late 1980s and into the 1990s became adept at branding their outsourced mass-produced running shoes and sports gear as embodying 'edgy' but healthy lifestyle choices, driven by a central idea of self-realization through decisive action (*'Just do it'*). By hiring stylish directors too such as Fincher (whose pulsing 1992 ad for Nike used John Lennon's 'Instant Karma' as backing track), and also Spike Lee (who appeared in his own series of ads for the Air Jordan shoe), Nike could add a sense of aesthetic kudos, while also, in their association with athletes like Michael Jordan and Tiger Woods, appearing to speak both for and to racial diversity. Such ads can be 'cool' by not specifically selling a *product*, since this would be to offer the viewer a reflection of themselves as a consumer. Ads like the ones above therefore represent an *idea*. Or as Dave Trumbore describes it, with Fincher's 'Instant Karma' ad, which intercuts snippets of athletes in action with hieroglyphic stick-drawings of bodies, Nike 'sold the sizzle instead of the steak' (Trumbore 2020).

At one point during the House committee hearings to which Zuckerberg testified in 2018, a somewhat naïve senator asked the Facebook CEO how, since it did not charge its users, the company made its money. 'Senator, we run ads', Zuckerberg replied; a response later enshrined on staff members' tee-shirts (Levy 2020: 429). Zuckerberg's blunt admission acknowledged that ads, cool or not, *were* in fact paying for the party. But to keep the party going, Facebook, equally, would have to be about emphasizing the 'sizzle', since they could not be seen to be selling the steak. As David Kirkpatrick wrote in 2010, trying hard to avoid the answer Zuckerberg gave eight years later,

> the word *advertising* is no longer really the right word for what's going on at Facebook. It is merely a useful shorthand ... to refer

to a process in which companies spend money to get people more interested in their products. (2010a: 263; emphasis in the original)

In other words, Facebook circa 2010 was finding itself in the quandary of trying to be a global-scale, growth-oriented business without doing the typical things, such as advertise, which helped to fund and enable growth: the same quandary that *The Social Network* dramatises. As Facebook's COO Sheryl Sandberg put it, after coming into the role in 2008, advertising typically dominates or at least alters the look of a website, but for Sandberg, ads 'should be good *experiences*, consistent with the good experience you were having on Facebook' (Levy 2020: 199–200, emphasis added).

For Mark in *The Social Network*, it is never *apparently* about the money, and yet it always is – just without explicitly saying so. Mark tells the Harvard Connection team he refused a purchase offer from Microsoft for his MP3 app, but instead 'uploaded it for free'. Divya's response – a flatly incredulous 'Why?' – seems more a rhetorical question than one inviting an explanation. Mark answers with a silent shrug. But the money it turns out is always a factor when it comes to developing and extending the reach of Facebook:

MARK: I need a dedicated Linux box running Apache with a MySQL backend. It's gonna cost a little more money.
EDUARDO: How much more?
MARK: Two-hundred more.
EDUARDO: Do we need it?
MARK: Gotta handle the traffic.
EDUARDO: Do it.
MARK: I already did.

Or later:

MARK: That reminds me, we're gonna need more money, Wardo.
EDUARDO: Yeah, no, I agree. More servers, more help
MARK: I'm interviewing two interns to come to Palo Alto and we're gonna have to pay them something.
EDUARDO: What?
MARK: I already found a house for rent on a street two blocks from the Stanford campus. It's perfect and it's got a pool.

Indeed, in the interview sequence described earlier, such is the ebullience and noise around the scene that we might easily overlook the moment Eduardo slips Mark an envelope: a personal contribution of $18,000 to 'get [Mark] through the summer' in his Palo Alto summer house (plus pool). What Eduardo sees as Mark's indifference to money, or even his naiveté with regard to its value, in effect represents part of Eduardo's own blindness to what is actually going on. In the contract-signing that leads, eventually, to the drastic dilution of Eduardo's stock value, the Facebook lawyer notes that Mark has reduced his own share of stock from 60% to 51%; to which news, Eduardo replies that Mark 'doesn't care about money' and that he 'needs to be protected'. Yet after Eduardo, feeling excluded from company decision-making, temporarily freezes the account that he himself is resourcing, Mark responds:

...	Do you realise that you jeopardized the entire company? Do you realise that your actions could have permanently destroyed everything I've been working on?
EDUARDO:	*We've* been working on.
MARK:	Without money, the site can't function.

Early on in the film, in fact, Mark has already demonstrated his own disingenuous attitude to wealth and the power it brings, when Eduardo's lawyer, Gretchen, suggests he dispossessed his former friend due to jealousy:

MARK:	[You're] suggesting I was jealous of Eduardo for getting punched by the Phoenix and began a plan to screw him out of a company I hadn't even invented yet.
GRETCHEN:	Were you?...
MARK:	Ma'am, I know you've done your homework and so you know that money isn't a big part of my life, but at the moment I could buy Mount Auburn Street, take the Phoenix Club and turn it into my ping-pong room.

As Mark's words reveal, his disregard for money has nevertheless left him 'at the moment' able to spend millions of his own dollars on property acquisitions, should he feel like it. And as the aforementioned examples also remind us, Facebook's success and Mark's abundant wealth is initially built on the outlay *not* of cool, but of capital – *Eduardo's* capital, to be precise, since neither Mark nor Sean have a sizeable amount to spare. Mark's lack of interest in money, it is worth reiterating, is also cushioned by the fact that, as a white, Harvard-attending male, and as a privileged member of the emerging Web 2.0 technocracy, he is already speaking from a position of security in which money does not *have* to be 'a big part' of his life, because it already is, and is always guaranteed. From which position, the only 'cool' thing to do, as far as money is concerned, is to disavow it – because he can afford to do so.

And the Weak (Ties) Will Inherit the Earth: The Cool Business of Web 2.0

To see one last time how a film like *Ferris Bueller's Day Off* informs one's understanding of *The Social Network*, it is useful to note that John Hughes' mid-eighties film depicts a form of primitive social network. A running joke in the movie is that everyone in the wider community seems to know Ferris, roots for him or helps him, without it ever being clear what he actually *does* either to make those connections or gain that trust.[10] The film's joke of course depends on a viewer's contextual awareness that no one could have that many friends or acquaintances – at least, before the era of the Internet. *Ferris Bueller* now seems inadvertently prescient in that it looked forward towards a time when the construction of such broad social networks would become both desirable and feasible; but it is also the very *vagueness* of what Ferris actually does, or wants to do, that gives the film some of its acuity ahead of the twenty-first century. While Ferris's imminent progression to college seems to be a given (a *cultural* given, since he happens to be white and economically advantaged), he seems to have no real idea nor interest in what he would actually study. Driscoll links the film to the contemporary 'entrepreneurial spirit' of Reaganomics, suggesting that the only real career Ferris can entertain is 'business' (2011: 53). Wondering exactly what this imprecise term means in the increasingly post-industrial 1980s, or why it might require a college degree, is precisely Driscoll's point, and as she notes, one of the many personae Ferris assumes during his day off is a broker at the Chicago stock exchange: a mover of invisible money. Yet a view of Ferris as entrepreneur, somewhat in the vein of Tom Cruise's Joel in *Risky Business*, or even Jim Sturgess's Ben in *21* (both discussed in Chapter 1), would overlook Ferris's real business skills. These lie not in his capacity to produce or sell anything, even in this case the products of his intellect. His skills lie rather in his more amorphous cultural savvy: his ability to know where to go, where to look, and above all, how to communicate this to others.

In youth films, we frequently see young protagonists trying and often failing to acquire the specific social and cultural acumen to survive their particular environments (Driscoll 2011: 59). This is a trait running through films such as *Sixteen Candles* (Hughes 1984), *The Breakfast Club*, *Heathers*, *Clueless*, *Cruel Intentions*, *Legally Blonde* (Luketic 2001), *Mean Girls*, *Superbad* and *Easy A*. We can see how these films are rarely just about 'high school' or 'college' per se, but in reality use these settings to stand in for the wider society into which their protagonists are set to emerge. What never changes through the genre, however, is the crucial significance of *popularity*: how to get it, maintain it, and how to respond when you lose it. In such cinematic contexts, being popular is a matter of social life or death.

For these protagonists, it is the mastery of social contexts and connections that matter as much, if not more, than mastering the school syllabus.[11] Ferris Bueller has no need for lessons in history and politics, but he *does* need the wider school and public body to provide meaning and value. Here, the emerging social network is already the market and economy of the future, and the commodity Ferris trades in is what is 'cool': artefacts, knowledge, original and differentiated kinds of experiences (indeed, in more contemporary parlance, and despite his lack of a beard, Ferris could clearly be identified as a 'hipster'). Ferris in many respects brings together the qualities Malcolm Gladwell, in his 2000 book *The Tipping Point*, identified as those of the 'Maven' and the 'Connector' (2000: 30–88): someone who knows what is 'happening', but who can also determine *what* happens, and how far it will extend, because of their extraordinary reach of contacts. These interconnected figures are the forces driving what Gladwell calls cultural 'epidemics': wildfire spreads of 'contagious' ideas, trends and fashions.

Sean Parker has said that the most important thing he ever did prior to Facebook was not founding Napster, but rather the work he did at Plaxo, 'developing algorithms for optimizing virality' (quoted in Fisher 2018: 350). Parker's real-life interest in virology and spreading ideas is keenly reflected in *The Social Network*. In a different film, and in a world where he did not exist in real life, Sean's cinematic entrance into Mark's world could almost be a parody of Bueller-like social networking and salesmanship. Justin Timberlake's performance is a finely tuned study in negotiating and owning not just space, but connections: watch the deftness with which he first appears to Mark and Eduardo, entering the upscale Chinese restaurant (in real life, the

recently opened 66 in Tribeca) to which he has invited the young entrepreneurs. Sean comes in, greeting, kissing and naming the female
staff as he does so, moving gracefully on light feet while pocketing his
sunglasses. Note also the way he precisely orders a series of *entrée*
dishes ('The lacquered pork with that ginger confit? Tuna tartar and a
lobster claws ...') without needing to look at a menu, because he already knows it by heart (a *Forbes* profile of Parker notes how, with the
Maven's immaculate attention to detail, Parker would dial ahead to
sushi restaurants to confirm 'which chef would be cutting the fish'
(Bertoni 2011)). Indeed, most commentators on the largely self-
educated Parker note how he appears to know something about almost *everything*: 'There is hardly a topic', writes David Kirkpatrick in
another profile piece, 'about which [Parker] cannot offer an informed
and nuanced opinion' (Kirkpatrick 2010b). From the start, then, Sean
displays the power of cultural knowledge and connections. While, in
reality, Parker barely had enough money in his bank account to cover
the cheque for his lunch with Mark (Kirkpatrick 2010a: 47),
Timberlake's Sean acts like the restaurant belongs to him; in much the
same way that, according to Eduardo's testimony in the film, he
'owned' Mark on the back of the meeting.

Parker's autodidact reading naturally extended to *The Tipping
Point*, topping his email invitations to Facebook's millionth-user
party with the book's final line: 'Look at the world around you. With
the slightest push – in just the right place – it can be tipped' (Gladwell
2000: 259; quoted in Kirkpatrick 2010a: 103). The key difference in
the end between Ferris Bueller and Sean, though, is that for all the
charismatic influence the latter might have on Mark in *The Social
Network*, he is not the star of the film – notably, the film's plot
provides a means to sideline him before its conclusion, when his
antics lead to his exclusion from Facebook's now very public face. As
with *Ferris Bueller*, what marks *The Tipping Point* as a product of the
previous, pre-Web 2.0 century is that it does not deal with the implications of the Internet – even if, like Hughes' film, Gladwell's book
hints at how the Internet will eventually be used. Ferris Bueller, in
person or as an image, is the star attractor in his particular network,
but the ultimate lesson of *The Social Network* is that such stars may
be superfluous. If viral ideas still need a 'slightest push' it is no longer
so evident that they need charismatic or well-connected individuals,
like Sean, to help them along. You do not even need *friends*.
Gladwell's study notes how Connectors are above all skilled at exploiting the strength of casual *acquaintances*, or 'weak ties'. 'Your
friends, after all, occupy the same world that you do', writes

Gladwell, stressing the lack of influence and viral power such 'strong' ties afford. 'How much, then, would they know that you wouldn't know?' (2000: 54). By contrast, and by definition, your circle of 'weak ties' represents a different set of social spheres and connections from the one you know, as well as offering connectivity to *their* networks of acquaintance: 'Acquaintances, in short, represent a source of social power, and the more acquaintances you have the more powerful you are'. Hence the power of the Connector, on whom we rely 'to give us access to opportunities and worlds to which we don't belong.' (ibid.)

This last thought is reminiscent of some of the statements made by Mark in his opening conversation about Final Clubs:

[Final Clubs are] *exclusive*. And fun, and they lead to a better life ... If I get in [to a Final Club] I'll be taking you ... to the events, and the gatherings ... and you'll be meeting a lot of people you wouldn't normally get to meet.

Yet the most significant line in the conversation, as usual, comes from Erica when she says:

The [Final Club] that's the easiest to get into would be the one where anybody has the best chance.

Alongside the rise in Web 2.0 connectivity, 'access to opportunities', as Gladwell puts it, is no longer prescribed by gatekeepers in the way that Final Clubs are, with their reliance on strong ties of class, wealth, and (the film quietly suggests) ethnicity or religion. Social network sites thrive by their very essence on the accumulation of more and more *weak* ties, many of them unseen but no less important for that fact. Within the logic of *The Social Network*, Facebook comes to embody precisely what Erica, with a simple democratic logic, imagines: a club where anybody has the best chance to get in, and anybody, or *everybody*, can be the President.

Parker recognized the importance of 'optimizing virality' since, in the emerging field of social networks, virality would be a way to prompt and maximize the sharing of information and ideas. The simple but far-reaching insight of Parker and Shawn Fanning, his partner at Napster, was that this virality would be intensified specifically by the lifestyle habits and interests of the young, and that a major cultural shift would be shaped not by influential individuals but by a dorm-room culture of other like-minded, digitally native high-schoolers and college students (Fisher 2018: 286–8). At the heart of Facebook's extraordinary take-up is what, for some, remains a counter-intuitive idea: that people might actually *want* to share personal information about themselves with other people online. An insight into Facebook's development, though, was that this was *exactly* what young people wanted to do. The new technological possibilities for users to author their own life online, rather than simply access and read content, was key to this transformation. As Steven Johnson comments, it was the emergence of blogging in particular, and the 'personal' links that this culture and such tools afforded, that changed the communicative possibilities of the Internet in its 2.0 phase, transforming it from a series of 'pages' to a user-oriented space (quoted in 349–50). For Johnson, Facebook eventually transcended its identity as merely 'a service or an app', becoming by the time of its billionth user 'a fundamental platform, on the same scale as the Internet itself' (quoted in 370).

Sean's eventual role in *The Social Network* is not, then, to be the star of the show, but simply to connect what is already a connection in progress. Sean is first seen waking in a Stanford dorm room, glimpsing a girl's Facebook page on her laptop. Fincher and Sorkin's film is not interested in showing how Facebook got there; just as it does not care to tell us, sometime later, when Cameron and Tyler race at the Henley Regatta, how it has made its way to the UK. It just *is*, as if a product of natural growth and expansion. The film is rarely interested either in showing what anyone is actually *doing* with the site: its own presence, and connection to other people, is apparently sufficient in itself. The functionality of Facebook is, of course, not its obvious USP, but rather the fact of its being linked to a massive set of weak ties. At the fateful millionth-member party in *The Social Network*, the huge enumerator on the screen is counting up to a number of users that is as ephemeral as it is impressive, with Sean, suitably, leading the call to 'Refresh!' (Figure 3.2). It is the *fact* of the number as a massive figure that is impactful; but it can only ever be an incredible fact and nothing more, since such a huge number is inevitably 'weak'; its scale overwhelming any idea of who these million users actually are, let alone how they might be using the site.

Notably, this key moment, and in some respects, the film's dramatic conclusion, takes place in the new home of Facebook: its second, expanded office on 156 University, Palo Alto. The décor, echoing Facebook's trademark blue and white, with the company logo

Figure 3.2 Enumerating Facebook's weak ties.

dominating, encapsulates the final transition of Facebook from its dorm-room and frat-house origins to its fully realized status as a major, and soon to be global, company. Presided over by Sean, while Mark remains plugged in at his laptop, the company is now on its way to the billion-dollar evaluation Sean foresaw. Facebook is now, to reiterate Sean's earlier words, officially cool by his monetary standards of the term. But at what costs? Appropriately, Fincher and Sorkin use this setting to show the demise of the film's main, indeed only, 'strong tie': the one formerly existing between Mark and Eduardo, the latter now crushed by his massive devaluation within the company's interests. In the aftermath of the party, it also provides the moment that Mark opens the box of business cards ordered, as the film suggests, at Sean's bidding: cards reading, simply, 'I'm CEO, Bitch'.[12] Sean makes this earlier suggestion for Mark amidst the seductive lights and equally seductive clientele of a downtown club, a techno track pulsing behind his spiel, as he dazzles Facebook's young founder with tales of ambition and power. The final revelation of the business cards, by contrast, comes in silence, with Mark alone in the now emptied offices.

The previous chapter already suggested how the film's final images may recall the ending of *Citizen Kane*, albeit with the skyscrapers of the West Coast replacing the secluded palace of Kane's Xanadu. From one perspective, *The Social Network*'s ending has a similarly moralizing message to the one that concludes Welles and Mankiewicz's film, though also one inflected by this later film's situation within the Web 2.0 economy. The strains of The Beatles' 'Baby, You're a Rich Man' build up slowly on the soundtrack as Mark, Erica Albright's Facebook page open before him, his face impassive and unreadable, repeatedly hits 'Add Friend' in hopeful and hopeless pursuit of his ex-girlfriend's attention. Meanwhile, a series of over-layered titles reveals the contemporary circumstances of Facebook and its founder: 'Facebook has 500 million members in 207 countries. It's currently valued at 25 billion dollars … Mark Zuckerberg is the youngest billionaire in the world'. For all the obviously intended irony in this disjuncture between text, music and Mark's on-screen actions, the film's final images powerfully assert the new ubiquity and normalization of Facebook as a means of communication, with Erica's simultaneous immediacy and distance a symptom of the tantalising world Mark has worked to create. Unlike Kane, who effectively builds an impenetrable wall between himself and the world, Mark has helped make the world more transparently available. What it all *means*, though, and what is its ultimate value to Mark, or indeed anyone, are questions the film leaves open. My concluding chapter looks at some of the responses.

Notes

1 Notably, *Rebel Without a Cause* was used as a key intertexual point of reference as recently as 2017, in *La La Land* (Chazelle), which quotes a sequence from the film and uses one of its key locations.

2 It is a perhaps inadvertent but notable aspect of the film's use of Coolio's track that Tai (Brittany Murphy) actually misquotes the song ('Rollin with *the* Homies') when she sings a refrain during the film.

3 These riots followed the filmed beating (in early 1992) of a black motorist, Rodney King, by white police officers, and the officers' subsequent acquittal.

4 My DVD of *The Social Network* has a photo of these slides, on the end of Mark's shorts-clad legs, behind the disc holder: an indication as to how important this aspect of costume design is to the film.

5 As Levy notes, Mark Zuckerberg has a closet full of near-identical T-shirts, all made by the designer Brunello Cucinelli, retailing at $325 each (Levy 2020: 1).

6 Eduardo's real sin, in fact, is probably to wear the *wrong* suit and to lack the proper accessories. A *Forbes* magazine portrait of Parker, published the year after *The Social Network* (Bertoni 2011), shows the entrepreneur in a sharp grey three-piece tailored by New York couturier Dashnor Begaj, offset by a pair of slightly scuffed, red Converse basketball shoes.

7 It is a contradiction running, subsequently, through Facebook's early culture. As Zuckerberg's Harvard roommate Chris Hughes told the *New Yorker* in 2006, one of the early Harvard-based groups on Facebook was called Not a Corporate Whore: many of its same members, Hughes notes, were also enthusiastic members of a fan group for Apple (Cassidy 2006).

8 The ad is quoted in *Steve Jobs*, played in the background as part of Jobs' unveiling of the new computer.

9 Huerta and Chavez were labour leaders and activists who together founded the National Farm Workers Association (NFWA); Chisholm, who in 1972 became the first African-American to seek the Presidential nomination, had in 1968 become the first black woman elected to the US Congress.

10 As Principal Rooney's secretary, Grace, reminds him, Ferris '[is] very popular ... The sportos, the motorheads, geeks, sluts, bloods, waistoids, dweebies, dickheads – they all adore him. They think he's a righteous dude'.

11 This is an idea wittily explored in the more recent *Booksmart*, which calls into question the value of academic application, when its two scholarly protagonists discover their hard-partying classmates have been accepted into Ivy League colleges and – in one case – been offered a six-figure starting-salary job at Google.

12 Whether or not Parker in real life made the suggestion, it remains a fact that Zuckerberg used this business card in Facebook's earliest years (Levy 2020: 88).

4 You Don't Get to Two Billion Friends Without Making a Few More Enemies: Critical Legacies of *The Social Network*

If one is generous, they might say that the years since *The Social Network* was released have not been kind to Facebook. The more honest truth, perhaps, is that Facebook has not been kind to these years. While the company's growth during the following decade made the original tagline's reference to 500 million users look under-ambitious, Facebook's credentials, not to mention the credibility of its CEO, have taken a battering. Among other examples of global misinformation, after the election of Donald Trump in the 2016 US presidential elections, Facebook was identified as having provided a platform for the viral spreading of fake news stories ('Hillary Clinton in 2013: "I Would Like to See People Like Donald Trump Run for Office"'), placed by proponents, motivated by either economic or political gain, skilled at exploiting the site's News Feed algorithms (Levy 2020: 334–67). Mark Zuckerberg played down the significance of such incidents, reverting to his core belief in Facebook's greater 'mission' (360–1).

The subsequent revelations that as many as 87 million Facebook users had effectively had their data stolen by a company called Cambridge Analytica (whose vice-president, Steve Bannon, would become a Trump advisor), proved harder to play down; especially since during this time Facebook never informed any of these users 'that their personal information had been operationalized – and their own News Feeds [subsequently] manipulated – for political purposes' (Levy 2020: 421). This led to what was, for the Facebook CEO, the apparently chastening appearance of testifying before Congressional committees in 2018, where he apologized for not 'do[ing] enough to prevent [Facebook's] tools from being used for harm' and for not 'tak[ing] a broad enough view of our responsibility'.

Zuckerberg's prepared statement at the hearings nevertheless began with a familiarly utopian refrain: 'Facebook is an idealistic and

DOI: 10.4324/9781003161936-5

optimistic company … focused on all the good connecting people can bring' (quoted in Levy 2020: 429). This was a few months before a white supremacist gunman entered a mosque in Christchurch, New Zealand, killing fifty-one worshippers, and streaming the whole thing on Facebook Live: a film viewed in real time by only a couple of hundred people but – more disturbingly – one that another 1.5 million users tried to upload, despite Facebook's attempt to erase it (443–4).

Facebook, moreover, even if people still use it, is no longer 'cool'; its reputation, especially among the young, tarnished by high-profile incidents like the ones above. Nor is Facebook any longer seen as an obvious employment destination for young computer-science graduates, potentially 'for moral reasons', while even employees from *within* Facebook raised doubts about its notional global role: in 2017, for example, only *half* of the employees quizzed said they believed 'that Facebook was good for the world' (Levy 2020: 472). Speaking at Stanford the same year, venture capitalist Chamath Palihapitiya, a former Facebook executive, described his one-time company as responsible for 'ripping apart the social fabric', and most tellingly of all, revealed that even his own children 'aren't allowed to use that shit' (quoted in Levy 2020: 473–4).[1]

Most recently, a *New Yorker* appraisal by Harvard historian Jill Lepore of Facebook's self-touted 'mission statement' – a statement Lepore concisely summarizes as 'baloney' – concludes with the telling assessment of Facebook's impact on the last decade:

> During the years of the company's ascent, the world has witnessed a loneliness epidemic, the growth of political extremism and political violence, widening political polarization, the rise of authoritarianism, the decline of democracy, a catastrophic crisis in journalism, and an unprecedented rise in propaganda, fake news and journalism. By no means is Facebook responsible for these calamities, but evidence implicates the company as a contributor to each of them. (Lepore 2021)

Quite a legacy.

Have the intervening years been as mixed for *The Social Network*? Possibly. As noted in my Introduction, I chose not to look in great detail at some of the contemporary critical responses to the film, mostly for the simple reason that they are all too visible. But more to the point, looking at responses to the film on the part of the more established film-critical community is somewhat incidental to this book's concerns with *The Social Network* as 'youth' film. In other words, the opinion of a consensus of film critics, such as the eighty-five contributors from *Sight & Sound* magazine who collectively chose *The Social Network* as 2010's film of the year, tells us only that Fincher and Sorkin's film meets the approval of that particular magazine's avowed *auteur*-cinema leanings. What it does not tell us, to put it bluntly, is whether the film means a thing to a younger generation the film makes some claims to represent, but who are under-represented in this same poll. Indeed, as many critics' polls as *The Social Network* might have topped in 2010 (Wikipedia gives the figure as twenty-two), given the kind of highbrow cinematic company in which the film is being put, one might ask – as I did at the beginning of this book – whether *The Social Network* is really a 'youth' film at all.[2]

Rather than simply list and resume a set of available critical views, then, I want in this final chapter to focus on a number of distinct responses to *The Social Network*; some contemporary with its release, others reflecting on the film at a later point, but many of them, significantly, coming from commentators whose response is often ambivalent, or indeed negative. These responses also tend to come from viewers much closer in generational terms to the young protagonists, rather than the middle-aged writer and director, of *The Social Network*. Admittedly, this remains a very narrow selection of responses: it is not within the scope or aims of this particular book to do an exhaustive survey. My aim here, instead, is to highlight some of the complexities involved when considering *The Social Network* as a film speaking to youth; but also, to look at the way the film's reputation is to some extent coloured by the parallel fortunes of the company whose creation it describes.

One has only to perform a Google search for 'The Social Network ten years later' (full disclosure: I did exactly this, as research for this current chapter) to see how many decade-on reflections exist within either the mainstream press, niche media or the blogosphere. *The Social Network* is not unique in this regard, but just a quick overview of many of these reflections highlights to what extent the film's legacy is bound up with the evolving attitudes towards Facebook, and above all, to public perceptions of its CEO. Eliciting such reactions is one of the risks of making a film about something not just as vast and influential as Facebook, but also about a historical context that in 2010 was still an expanding and developing one. Entirely fictional films with fictional characters, by virtue of their very status as inventions, remain relatively protected from retrospective scrutiny. While the racial and sexual politics of John Hughes' films have come in for criticism over the years, I don't personally know anyone who holds *Ferris Bueller's*

Day Off to account for its lack of realism. Such is the ubiquity of both Facebook and Zuckerberg in the public eye, though, that it seems difficult, for some, to separate the fiction from the emerging facts.

Kaitlyn Tiffany's (2017) piece in *The Verge*, for instance, part of a series of reviews revisiting older films, argues that *The Social Network*, despite still being 'one of the sharpest movies I've ever seen', now 'feels like a relic, a naïve movie with quaint, softball critiques of Mark Zuckerberg and his creation'. Tiffany's reserve around the film appears to stem from the fact that *The Social Network* under-estimated Facebook's own reach and impact: the fact, for example, that Sean's promise of 'a billion dollars', even in 2010, after the kinds of sums deployed to save failing US banks just a year previously, would 'sound like nearly nothing'; or the way Sean's supposedly 'impressive, seductive' reaching out to Mark – 'They're scared of me, pal, and they're going to be scared of you' – jars in the light of the more recent concerns about the masculine culture of Silicon Valley.

The film's supposedly uncritical fascination with its central protagonist, as well as its disregard for any substantial female characters – the bookending figures of Erica and Marylin notwithstanding – also earns the film its detractors, with Sonia Saraiya's (2020) revisiting in *Vanity Fair* taking particular aim. As she puts it, Sorkin's script 'invents several excuses to show coeds in their underwear ... [while] Harvard women who are not wearing thigh-high boots and eyeliner simply do not exist in the film'. Saraiya is also not alone in highlighting some of the liberties the film takes with historical truth: the fact, as she notes, that Facemash actually included male photos as well as female ones; or that Zuckerberg was in fact in a relationship with Priscilla Chan, his future wife, at the time he invented Facebook, thereby skewing the film's view of Mark as a 'horny nerd misogynist' (Saraiya 2020).

While Saraiya also argues that the more negative aspects of Facebook, especially in terms of the anomie and anxiety it engenders in many of its users, was already well evidenced by 2010, there is still a sense of retrospective mapping in these responses. In other words, for such detractors, the film's shortcomings lie in its failure to adequately anticipate the future. This temptation to see the film as a 'prescient' one, or conversely, to criticize its *lack* of prescience, is one that *Rolling Stone*'s David Fear has cautioned against, arguing that we see Fincher and Sorkin's film one decade on simply as 'chronicl[ing] a certain subset of Ivy-League entitlement and Cali tech-bro culture' (Fear 2020). Fear nevertheless highlights that, while in 2010, 'it was still ever-so-slightly possible to consider Mark Zuckerberg "the little guy" in this scenario', the kinds of cultures the film described 'had already wreaked plenty of social havoc' (ibid.). Indeed, part of Saraiya's reservations centre on the fact that *before* 2010, Facebook was already starting to exploit its users' data in unforeseen ways: 'The great tragedy of *The Social Network*', she writes, 'is that Eduardo and Mark's friendship is damaged by Mark's greed; the great tragedy of Facebook though, is that Zuckerberg *sold out his users for profit*' (Saraiya 2020, emphasis in the original).

Suitably enough, criticism of *The Social Network*'s historical acuity has not just come retrospectively, since the film has also been seen as misrepresenting both its contemporary moment and its then quite recent past. Writing at the time of *The Social Network*'s release, in one of the more conspicuously negative reviews of the film, Nathan Heller takes to task what he sees as its over-exaggeration of Harvard's social stratifications, and its vision of Final Clubs as propagators of an Old School network. Speaking from his experience as one of Zuckerberg's contemporaries at Harvard, Heller argues that Final Clubs

> were seen as basically vestigial curios, removed from the main artery of the school's cultural life: The notion that a crack Web programmer in 2003 would find his future blocked off by their fusty gatekeeping is risible ... [Facebook] didn't rise as a scrappy force trying to conquer a patrician culture. That culture was already dead. Its rituals were theater. Any paths that may once have existed were now overgrown or paved and clotted with pedestrians all headed to the promised land. (Heller 2010)

Heller's point, appropriately, is echoed in Ali Leskowitz's (2010) otherwise enthusiastic review from the *Harvard Crimson*, which questions the orgiastic depictions of 'Harvard's semi-secret all-male social organizations'. Significantly, though, Leskowitz, who argues that Sorkin's script 'nails Harvard's unique vernacular', reminds us that the Final Clubs as shown in the film 'are hardly presented as the objective pinnacles of Harvard's social life', adding moreover that 'only the Zuckerberg of the movie sees them that way'. This is an important reminder of the way *The Social Network* is structured as a story narrated by the protagonists of the film, not from some notionally omniscient outsider. Once one starts digging up the film's inaccuracies, one loses sight not only of its status as fiction, but more specifically, its status as a story told from a series of particular, subjective points of view.

Sorkin has always justified his approach as one that privileges dramatic value over historical truth, and in an alternate universe where

Facebook did not (yet) exist, one might well view *The Social Network* simply as a great piece of imaginative, dramatic filmmaking: a study of class and culture, resentment, ambition and the force of an idea. If the team at Facebook had had their way – they requested that the company never be named and the protagonists' names altered – this might well have been the case (Harris 2010). It follows that, by at least insisting on naming names and places, not to mention drawing from information existing in the public record, the film subjects itself to scrutiny: not, necessarily, for its attention to specific detail, but at least, for its capacity to adequately capture the atmosphere of the time. After all, it is on this broader social and cultural canvas that the film's drama depends, and for Heller, the film's shortcoming is its over-dramatization of these perspectives themselves:

> What Facebook really gave us, for better or worse, was a new social and intellectual culture that *we could claim*, finally, *as our own*. During its early rise, the site allowed the social flavor of the Ivy League to include more than just playing dress-up and pretend. (We now played those games online, as our own.) These days, it's helped open a large, uncharted territory for a generation whose world first seemed, in many ways, competitively tighter and more predetermined than ever. (Heller 2010, emphasis in the original)

There is an inherent irony here, though, that Heller fails to note, which is that *The Social Network* appears outdated not because it gets things wrong, but because the change it dramatizes *has already happened*. Heller shows a somewhat proprietorial take on assessing the film's subject matter, which claims authority on the basis that the reviewer attended Harvard in the early 2000s: here was 'an intellectual culture that w*e could claim … as our own*'. Whether or not one holds with the film's schematic depiction of Harvard's social hierarchies, *The Social Network*'s whole narrative context is the ushering in of this new 'intellectual culture', to the point where it becomes, simply, a way of life. The banality and normalization of Facebook by 2010 and beyond, but more importantly, the fact that it is now a ubiquitous part of culture, might render *The Social Network* a film stuck in the past, but if one is laughing about its dramatization of this past now – or even in 2010 – is it not because we have been living all this time in the world whose infancy the film is describing? To take issue with *The Social Network* for its failure to grasp 'our' intellectual culture is in some respects to acknowledge the film's accuracy in narrating this major generational shift.

Whose 'Social Network' Is It Anyway?

Heller also seems to overlook his own position of privilege within the discussion. Chastising *The Social Network* for failing to grasp the nature and character of social media culture up to and including 2010 is in effect to take the position of Facebook 'natives' or early adopters. But in some respects, this same position carries its own problems. Heller claims the culture of social media as '*our own*', but this implied 'we' is potentially very narrow rather than universal in its assumptions. This is a point picked up in another revisiting of the film, this time from Megan Garber in *The Atlantic*. Garber highlights Zuckerberg's Harvard commencement address of 2017, in which the Facebook CEO – in one configuration of his 'mission statement' – re-worked a famous phrase from the civil rights movement to strangely self-serving ends: 'We understand the great arc of human history bends towards people coming together in ever greater numbers', Zuckerberg stated, adding that his own 'story' was one of 'connecting one community at a time, and keeping at it until one day we can connect the whole world' (quoted in Garber 2019). As Garber retorts:

> Who is the "we" in that formulation? What is "the whole world"? There are reflections of the Gilded Age in this era of digital expansion—extreme wealth, restive people, new structures being grafted onto the ones that were already there.

Garber's subsequent view on the value of *The Social Network* is to view it not as biography, but as an encapsulation of a world determined by this 'we', and 'what it will mean for people to live lives that are conducted, at least in part, online'; a world built by 'a small collection of people, appointed first by chance and then by themselves, attempting to decide for the rest of us what it means, finally, to connect'. From this perspective, the film's seemingly obscure focus on one problematic individual and a small group of associates is precisely its broader dramatic and thematic point.

Other critics, either returning to the film or writing at the time of release, reflect this same uncertainty regarding their own generational or spiritual place in the film's 'world'. Leonardo Goi, in a reappraisal for MUBI's *Notebook* website, suggests that while he and Zuckerberg, separated by just six years, 'belong to the same generation', their worlds 'couldn't be more different'; going on to say that the film's depiction of Mark and his Facebook colleagues is to him 'so alien … they may as well all belong to some unknown Amazon tribe' (Goi 2018).

Another view of simultaneous closeness and dislocation is offered by novelist Zadie Smith, who acknowledges – jokily – that she was 'there' at the birth of Facebook in 2003, as a Harvard research fellow; before adding that, while only nine years older than Zuckerberg, 'somehow it doesn't feel that way' (Smith 2010). *Almost* young enough to be a contemporary of the Harvard undergraduates at the time, and located at the epicentre of Facebook's eruption into university and social life, Smith is nevertheless *not quite* at the right age or in the right place:

> I still feel distant from [the kids at Harvard] now, ever more so, as I increasingly opt out (by choice, by default) of the things they have embraced. We have different ideas about things. Specifically we have different ideas about what a person is, or should be. I often worry that my idea of personhood is nostalgic, irrational, inaccurate. Perhaps Generation Facebook have built their virtual mansions in good faith, in order to house the People 2.0 they genuinely are, and if I feel uncomfortable within them it is because I am stuck at Person 1.0. (Smith 2010)

Smith's uneasy positioning on the fringes of People 2.0, combined with a critical sense that the latter remains a self-elected and elite group, is echoed in a 2020 *New York Times* retrospective by the poet and journalist Maya Phillips (a college undergraduate at the time of the film's release). Phillips notes how *The Social Network*, perhaps un-knowingly (via the Facemash sequence), pointed to how Facebook in the future 'would manipulate personal data', but also to 'how solitary it could actually make users feel'. Like Garber, she also picks up on the ironies built into the film, against the backdrop of Mark's bid for 'connectivity': the way the film, ultimately, is not about being con-nected at all, but focuses exclusively on a 'social domain' that is 're-markably small': an enclave of 'white, privileged man-children'. As she notes, the film in the end is about the founding of an enterprise and little else: something we 'buy into' and which, experience since 2010 has told us, 'has proved that [Facebook is] not simply the innocent model of social connection that the real Zuckerberg has made it out to be'. Even the film's title, in its functional descriptiveness and ab-straction, 'gestures at the professional, impersonal connotations of [such] systems' (Phillips 2020).

These various responses to the film encapsulate a perspective on *The Social Network* that sees its significance not in terms of historical accuracy but in its dramatic capacity to capture the sense of a coming or already evolved world. What Fincher and Sorkin's film offers, in this view, is a suggestion of what the world starts to *feel* like once Facebook has made its influence felt, not only its extraordinary capacity to become part of our lives but also its *in*capacity to make up for age-old human needs and desires. The Mark seen at the end of *The Social Network* is not the 'real' Mark Zuckerberg, but does that matter? It is the crushing sense of disconnection that provides the force of the scene, as Mark is left alone, too legally thorny – or perhaps just too toxic – to be touched. The lawyers, without him, have gone out for a steak dinner: Mark does not even know where they are. When Mark asks Marylin, who is still there, if she wants to get a bite, her answer – a resigned 'I can't' – tells us that Mark is off-limits. As Goi notes, efforts to praise or blame the film for being either prophetic or damning – both, as I have suggested, unhistorical and retrospective takes on the film – miss the point. *The Social Network*'s power

> does not reside so much in the prophecies nestled inside it, but in the way it understands how a friendship can crumble under the weight of ambition, betrayal and jealousy. Its climax is not Facebook's million members party, but that line [Eduardo] tells [Mark] with imploring disbelief in an earlier courtroom deposition: 'I was your only friend. You had *one* friend'. (Goi 2018)

Not that this argument washes with other commentators on the film. Both Saraiya and Tiffany have criticized what they see as *The Social Network*'s ultimate recourse to a story about Mark and the search for his humanity. The story and its implications, for them, are much too big for this. For Tiffany, in its decision to focus on its founder's personal drama, the film misses the point that at a profound level this is not just about Mark, but about everyone. 'Zuckerberg isn't a villain because he treated some people badly when he was 20 years old', summarizes Tiffany: 'he's a villain because he's one of the most powerful people alive, and nobody asked him to be' (Tiffany 2017). But as I have argued in this book, is this not exactly what *The Social Network* is trying to show? The film is as much about the cultural and technological circumstances that allow for Facebook to happen, as it is a portrait of unique and isolated genius. No one *asked* Mark Zuckerberg to be one of the most powerful men alive, but if he is, it is because *people chose to use Facebook*, and not because they were told to.

The focus on the (invented) character of Erica Albright as a 'Rosebud' figure in the film is, moreover, as potentially irrelevant as the fixation with Rosebud itself – what turns out to be the protagonist's lost childhood sled – in *Citizen Kane*: a false trail, a deliberate simplification of a story far more complex than such easy psychological explanations allow. *The Social Network* dramatizes the point at which recklessness and narrow, personal narratives, within the reshaped politics and economies of Web 2.0, interweave with power; and when billions are to be made, and country-eclipsing companies to be founded, regardless or not of whether anyone 'asked'. To go back to the quote that began this book: it's about what happens when we let kids build companies with no boundaries, in their own image.

Suggesting, moreover, that the film washes over Mark's problematic actions in the pursuit of a humanizing narrative overlooks its specific concerns with responsibility and accountability. Does the whole structure of the film, in fact, in terms of its narration from the viewpoint of the litigation scenes, not underline that this is a film about *damage*? Focusing on what Erica supposedly does or does not do to Mark's soul also detracts attention from what is actually Mark's most egregious act in the film: the fact that he wrote about her in the first place. Later responses to *The Social Network* would no doubt be different if, instead of Marylin's softened criticism of Mark, the film had ended with the reprimand Erica dishes out to Mark earlier in the film:

> You called me a bitch on the internet, Mark ... On the *internet* ... As if every thought that tumbles through your head is so clever it would be a crime for it not to be shared. The internet's not written in pencil, Mark, it's written in ink and you *published* that Erica Albright was a bitch ...

Banality, idiocy, misogyny, converted into fact, into 'news', because it is online. This *is* part of the world Facebook created, but as Erica attests, it is already here in *The Social Network*. Garber's focus on the film's broader symbolic aspects highlights that its story is not unique, but is more representative of what happens when a specific youth culture – call it 'Silicon Valley', for simplicity's sake – is able to force the communications agenda. As she writes: 'Figuratively and sometimes literally, slightly beer-drunk college sophomores are deciding for the rest of us what, and who, matters. A few people, with all their quirks and contingencies, are shaping the spaces that summon us' (Garber 2019). Or as Smith similarly concludes, the film is in the end 'not a cruel portrait of any particular real-world person called "Mark Zuckerberg". It's a cruel portrait of us: 500 million sentient people entrapped in the recent careless thoughts of a Harvard sophomore' (Smith 2010). As Saraiya would have preferred, *The Social Network* might have been wider in its scope, offering more a view of what it is like to be among these 500 million people. That it chose not to be, I would argue, is not a deficiency of the film. By narrowing the action of the film down to its tiny cast of characters, the film makes the point more emphatically: from a group of kids *like these*, and from their idle, brilliant and careless thoughts and whims, we get *this*.

An Empire without Bounds

A 2010 feature on the Facebook CEO published in the *New Yorker*, just prior to the release of *The Social Network*, highlighted Zuckerberg's peculiarly double nature: someone at once interested in networking and democratizing the Internet, yet whose questioning of privacy had already raised concerns; along with his willingness, in terms of how his company exploited its users' data, to 'violate ... the social compact upon which the company [was] based' (Vargas 2010). More striking still is the portrait the feature paints of a still very young man oddly in touch with his exceptional role in history. As Sean Parker, quoted in the article, concurs, 'there was a part of [Mark] present even when he was twenty, twenty-one – this kind of imperial tendency'. On cue, in the course of the same interview, Zuckerberg discusses his admiration for the *Aeneid*, the ancient Latin epic, from which he quotes two of his favourite lines: 'Fortune favors the bold ... a[n] empire without bounds' (quoted in ibid.).

One might read too much into this. There are plenty of nineteen-year-old fans of classical poetry, and even more who, like Zuckerberg, also enjoy world-domination and empire-building games such as Risk and Civilization. Most of these, however, do not build empires in real life. The fact that Zuckerberg went from the former to the latter is less relevant for the reductive psychological and biographical assumptions drawn from it, and more for what it says about twenty-first-century life, and its distinctions from the worlds of Ancient Greece or Rome. Zuckerberg, we are told, was in his bedroom at his computer, playing Civilization, the moment he received his acceptance email from Harvard. Apparently, after briefly acknowledging this news, he re-turned to the game (Levy 2020: 38). As noted earlier, one of the main ideas evoked in *The Social Network* is that of a life increasingly, and then as a matter of course, lived online. Facebook's main impact, beyond its status as a directory of humanity, was to take the lead role in this transition of the Internet into a space of habitation and social interaction, but it emerged out of an idea that could be, and largely was, hatched out of a bedroom, written in code on the same devices that would connect us all. From playing Civilization to playing world domination via Facebook is not, in reality, such a huge leap, since they start and end in the same place.

The link between computing and empire-building is not a facetious one. As the historian Yuval Harari has argued, political power is essentially a question of how quickly data can be processed. For Harari, the key political transformation of the Internet age is the speed at which such processing can occur in comparison both with previous periods and other methods. Democratic institutions such as 'political parties and parliaments ... evolved in an era when politics moved faster than technology ... Yet whereas the rhythm of politics has not changed much since the days of steam, technology has switched from first gear to fourth. *Technological revolutions now outpace political processes*' (Harari 2015: 435–6, emphasis added). Instantaneity, virality, connectivity: we have already seen how these characteristics of twenty-first-century communication are highlighted by the narrative and style of *The Social Network*. The film understands this sense of how new empires are built from new sites and new agents, dislocated from 'politics' in its traditional sense, but no less political in its often troubling ramifications and impact.

Coincidentally, a *Vanity Fair* list identifying what it saw as the 100 most influential global figures, published the month of *The Social Network*'s release, anointed the then twenty-six-year-old Zuckerberg as 'our new Caesar' (Deutschmann et al. 2010). Whether or not the classics-loving CEO really does see his role as an emperor, to all intents and purposes he may as well be, given both Facebook's scale, and its capacity to convert idea into action and effect almost instantaneously. As we have seen, one of the key themes of *The Social Network* is the impact and permanence of actions made, often with no consideration of their repercussions, and more often than not at incredible speed (note that Erica appears to be the *last* person in her university building to hear she has been written about). The scale or intention of an action and its global impact no longer have an obvious correlation, and the inconsequential can have its consequences. This might be in the form of the fake or trivial stories that, positioned by Facebook's algorithms, constitute the most important story in your News Feed (explaining this new tool in 2006, Zuckerberg suggested, with no apparent irony, that '[a] squirrel dying in front of your house may be more relevant to your interests right now than people dying in Africa' (Kirkpatrick 2010a: 181)). Or, at a different level, it might be the imposition of the Facebook site itself, in terms of its very shape and form. As Vargas notes, Facebook's distinctive home pages have the blue colour only because Zuckerberg, who is red-green colour-blind, likes blue (2010). Consequently, as a 'Mark Zuckerberg Production', one sees blue when seeing or even thinking about Facebook. As random as this is, it is another instance of the contingent, but also the *personal*, shaping the world we live in: 'domination', only by a different means.

The negative and destructive aspects of this empire-building are hardly lost on *The Social Network*, which explores how Facebook divides as many people as it brings together. Mark's journey to become one of the world's most powerful men, at an age when others are just getting out of school, is littered with casualties, including, the film suggests, himself. And yet, at the possible risk of sounding glib, the film's other often-overlooked point is that *he actually did it*. When Goi asks what it is exactly that entices us about *The Social Network*, I suggest that it has to be much more than just universal dramatic themes, if only because these in themselves are not uniquely interesting. Whether we like it or not, Facebook – the creative ideas informing its infancy, its enormous scope and uptake – is remarkable, and it has come in large part to define the century in which we live. One cannot really make sense of the potential appeal of *The Social Network* without taking into account that simple fact.

Ultimately, I am not sure that the film speaks to the specific generation it (partially) depicts; or that it accurately represents, or is even interested in accurately representing, those same people whose lives it turns into fiction. Insofar as the film depicts the excitement of creating something new, I would nevertheless argue that *The Social Network* is unquestionably *about youth*, or more specifically, about *what it feels like to be young.* To return to the quotation from Fincher cited in this book's Introduction, the film depicts, for good or ill, 'what it is to be youthful and have a dream and enthusiasm'. As this chapter's overview has highlighted, from the vantage point of the present, or even from 2010, it is easy to take either *The Social Network* or Fincher's viewpoint to task, but this overlooks the grounds for the film's original success and appeal. It also fails to acknowledge the blunt fact underlying the film itself as a project: that Facebook, an invention with little precedent, should be taken up so enthusiastically by so many people, globally. Nor does it follow that to engage positively with the film, as so many did, is to uncritically embrace its protagonists. As I have stressed throughout this book, the answer, as always, is somewhere in between. This is a film that thrives on its *ambivalent* vision, not its univocal position on either side of the Facebook divide.

The Social Network, as I have shown, builds substantial ironies into its depictions of Facebook's creation, dwelling on the moral and epistemological abyss Facebook straddles, and the paradoxes inherent to what Facebook itself stands for. But as I have also argued, the film is equally invested in depicting the *energy* of this act of creativity – what it means to be young, reckless, and at the same time, to have a brilliant idea. The ambiguity of the whole film could be summed up in one single shot from early on, in which Mark and Eduardo, along with Dustin and Chris (Hughes), are shown leaning in towards Mark's screen as they try out the Facemash algorithm (Figure 4.1). Watching a group of males judging female hotness via hacked images is problematic, but the shot *also* captures the buzz of being young, making something new, in one's room, very late at night. To reiterate Fincher's other point, this is a film 'about kid's faces', and here, the youthful, eager faces tell us everything. 'It works', says Eduardo, appreciatively – if not a little warily – as he takes another glug from his plastic tumbler. *It works*. In those two words lies the simple spark that catches fire, becoming something so much bigger. The judgement, it leaves to us – the characters, for the most part, are having way too much fun.

Are they to be damned for this? History eventually might say yes, but on the evidence I have offered here, the film is more circumspect. It is not at all clear that *The Social Network* is asking its audience to sympathize or even empathize with its young protagonists. But as a film about *youth*, which is to say, ultimately, a film about being

Figure 4.1 'It works'.

modern, and therefore about generational *difference*, is that not part of the point? Or alternatively – as I suspect might tacitly lie, unmentioned, behind some of the most rapturous responses to the film – does the film make some viewers nostalgically recall a similar youthful time in their lives, stirring the memory of creating something great with one's friends? Or again, might it even provoke a gentle tinge of envy? I can only leave this question to individual readers and viewers.

Smith captures the strange ambiguity of *The Social Network* when she suggests the film 'feel[s] more delightful than it probably, objectively, is' (Smith 2010). To reflect on Smith's point, the contradiction here relates to the way the story drives in two simultaneous and interweaving directions: on one side, the chronicle of a dubious enterprise shaped by people of questionable motivation; and on the other, the tale of a brilliant piece of technological and creative innovation, dreamt up by a cluster of very smart young people. The problem, as Smith notes, is neither the technology nor the generation in themselves, the problem is 'that some of the software currently shaping [the 2.0] generation is unworthy of them. They are more interesting than it is' (ibid.).

Notably, though, part of what makes them interesting is that they might also come up with something as unexpected, as *unprecedented*, as Facebook, thereby defining their own cultural and creative territory, set apart from the influence or judgements of others. Or as Smith eloquently puts it,

> this 2.0 generation [has] spent a decade being berated for not making the right sorts of paintings or novels or music or politics. Turns out the brightest 2.0 kids have been doing something else extraordinary. They've been making a world. (Smith 2010)

Lest we ever forget, *The Social Network* offers a memento of this fact, and of this extraordinary and complex moment in our history and culture.

Notes

1 Palihapitiya later retracted this remark, but he still said it.
2 To provide some context, *Sight & Sound* editor Nick James, in his preface to the 2010 poll results, and reflecting on the absence of mainstream US hits in the list, opines that 'the sort of cinema the wider public flocks to see … bears little relationship to what our 85 contributors want to celebrate'. Apart, of course, from their number one film; a fact he conveniently uses to prove that

the same contributors, despite their antipathy to mainstream film, are not 'hit-phobic' (James 2010). Within such critical contexts, *The Social Network* is celebrated *in spite of* its broader public success and is seen as an exception to the general rule in US filmmaking: in this case, as an 'auteur' film that also happened to be popular.

Epilogue: The Last Word?

In early October 2020, showbiz media briefly buzzed with the prospect of a sequel to *The Social Network*. Adding that Fincher would need to be back on board as director, it was Sorkin, in an interview on the *Happy.Sad.Confused* podcast, who mooted the possibility of returning to the Facebook story.[1] 'I do want to see it', Sorkin claimed. 'And [producer] Scott [Rudin] wants to see it … People have been talking to me about it. What we've discovered is the dark side of Facebook' (quoted in Couch 2020).

Critics of *The Social Network* might say Sorkin was ten years too late to this 'dark side'. It is clear, nevertheless, from Sorkin's wider concerns with Mark Zuckerberg and Facebook – notably, the open letter he published in the *New York Times* a year prior (Sorkin 2019) – that he understands his own responsibility in telling a part of the Facebook story. At the time of writing, one can only speculate what a *Social Network* sequel might be about, though Sorkin hints at a story involving shady subcommittee hearings on Facebook's threat to democracy. A flattering portrait of the Facebook CEO, should it happen, it promises not to be.

Who would be watching, though? Hollywood's risk-averse logic would suggest that a sequel to the $240 million-grossing original makes sense, yet even a sparkling Sorkin script for the similar-seeming *Steve Jobs* in 2015 could not save that critically praised film from commercial failure. Would audiences return to Sorkin and Fincher's Zuckerberg – older, a little paunchier, (even) more damaged and damaging – more than a decade on? I touched on the point previously that contemporary youth cinema has in many respects grown up with an audience that is now adult, looking back to (their) youth (Kaklamanidou 2018: 28). If *The Social Network*, as I have argued, offers a reminder of what it might feel like to be young, perhaps a sequel would merely remind its viewers how old they have eventually become.

Still, a follow-up to *The Social Network* might also offer an opportunity to both address and redress the issues raised by the original film. Maybe, it would also be a chance to depict the voices of the first truly *post-Facebook* generation, one seeking to revive or replace that company's forsaken ideals. Whether or not the film happens, we can only, quite literally, wait and see.

Note

1 The fact that Sorkin, rather than Fincher, appears to dictate the terms and possibilities of a sequel is one further indication that the screenwriter be seen as the 'author' of *The Social Network* (cf. Introduction, Note 1).

Bibliography

Abrams, N. (2012) *The New Jew in Film: Exploring Jewishness and Judaism in Contemporary Cinema*, London and New York: I.B. Tauris.

Archer, N. (2013) '*The Girl with the Dragon Tattoo* (2009/2011) and the New "European Cinema"', *Film Criticism*, Vol. 37, No. 2, pp. 1–20.

Archer, N. (2016) 'Speeds of Sound: On Fast Talking in Slow Movies', *Cinema Journal*, Vol. 55, No. 2, pp. 130–135.

Archer, N. (2017) '*Gone Girl* (2012/2014) and the Uses of Culture', *Literature/Film Quarterly*, Vol. 45, No. 3, https://lfq.salisbury.edu/_issues/45_3/gone_girl.html.

Archer, N. (2019) *Twenty-First-Century Hollywood: Rebooting the System*, London and New York, NY: Wallflower Press.

Bakhtin, M. (1984) *Rabelais and His World*, Bloomington, IN: Indiana University Press.

Barkhorn, E. (2010) 'Mark Zuckerberg on The Social Network's Biggest Flaw', *Atlantic*, online, 19 October, https://www.theatlantic.com/entertainment/archive/2010/10/mark-zuckerberg-on-the-social-networks-biggest-flaw/64786/.

Baron, C. and S. M. Carnicke (2008) *Reframing Screen Performance*, Ann Arbor, MI: The University of Michigan Press.

Bertoni, S. (2011) 'Sean Parker: Agent of Disruption', *Forbes*, online, 21 September, https://www.forbes.com/sites/stevenbertoni/2011/09/21/sean-parker-agent-of-disruption/?sh=6fe37b787000.

Blackmore, T. (2007) 'The Speed Death of the Eye', *Bulletin of Science, Technology & Society*, Vol. 27, No. 5, pp. 367–372.

Bordwell, D. (2006) *The Way Hollywood Tells It: Story and Style in Modern Movies*, Berkeley, CA: University of California Press.

Bordwell, D. (2011) 'THE SOCIAL NETWORK: Faces behind Facebook', *Observations on Film Art*, online, 30 January, http://www.davidbordwell.net/blog/2011/01/30/the-social-network-faces-behind-facebook/.

Bordwell, D. and K. Thompson (2004) *Film Art: An Introduction*, 7th edition, New York, NY: McGraw-Hill.

Broderick, M. (2007) 'Rebels with a Cause: Children Versus the Military Industrial Complex', in T. Shary and A. Seibel (eds), *Youth Culture in Global Cinema*, Austin, TX: University of Texas Press, pp. 37–55.

Brody, R. (2010) 'An Empire of His Own', *New Yorker*, online, 25 September, https://www.newyorker.com/culture/richard-brody/an-empire-of-his-own.

Brown, N. (2013) '"Family" Entertainment and Contemporary Hollywood Cinema', *Scope: An Online Journal of Film and Television Studies*, Vol. 25, online, https://www.nottingham.ac.uk/scope/documents/2013/february-2013/brown.pdf.

Browning, M. (2010) *David Fincher: Films that Scar*, Santa Barbara, CA and Denver, CO and Oxford: Praeger.

Buckland, W. (2009) (ed) *Puzzle Films: Complex Storytelling in Contemporary Cinema*, Chichester: Blackwell.

Carlson, N. (2012) 'EXCLUSIVE: Mark Zuckerberg's Secret IMs from College', *Business Insider*, online, 17 May, https://www.businessinsider.com/exclusive-mark-zuckerbergs-secret-ims-from-college-2012-5?r=US&IR=T.

Carr, N. (2008) 'Is Google Making Us Stupid?', *The Atlantic*, online, June/July, https://www.theatlantic.com/magazine/archive/2008/07/is-google-making-us-stupid/306868/.

Carr, N. (2011) *The Shallows: What the Internet Is Doing to Our Brains*, New York, NY and London: W.W. Norton.

Cartmell, D. and I. Whelehan (2010) *Screen Adaptation: Impure Cinema*, Basingstoke and New York, NY: Palgrave Macmillan.

Cassidy, J. (2006) 'Me Media', *New Yorker*, online, 7 May, https://www.newyorker.com/magazine/2006/05/15/me-media.

Chandra, V. (2013) *Geek Sublime: Writing Fiction, Coding Software*, London: Faber & Faber.

Chase, S. (2020) *Filminimalism: A Multi-Framework Analysis of Postminimalist Techniques in Contemporary Film Music. Embodied Cognition and Misempathetic Music in the Film Scores of Johann Johannsson, Trent Reznor and Atticus Ross, and Mica Levi*, Unpublished PhD Thesis, University of Surrey, https://openresearch.surrey.ac.uk/esploro/outputs/doctoral/Filminimalism-a-multi-framework-analysis-of-postminimalist/99513435702346.

Coker, M. (2007) 'Startup Advice for Entrepreneurs from Y-Combinator', *VentureBeat*, online, 26 March, https://venturebeat.com/2007/03/26/start-up-advice-for-entrepreneurs-from-y-combinator-startup-school/.

Collins, J. (2002) 'High-Pop: An Introduction', in J. Collins (ed) *High-Pop: Making Culture into Popular Entertainment*, Malden, MA and Oxford: Blackwell, pp. 1–32.

Considine, D. (1985) *The Cinema of Adolescence*, Jefferson, NC: McFarland.

Couch, A. (2020) 'Aaron Sorkin Would Like to Write "Social Network" Sequel', *Hollywood Reporter*, online, 7 October, https://www.hollywoodreporter.com/movies/movie-news/aaron-sorkin-would-like-to-write-social-network-sequel-4072910/.

Deutschman, A., P. Newcomb, R. Siklos, D. McDonald and J. Flint (2010) 'The *Vanity Fair* 100', *Vanity Fair*, online, 1 September, https://www.vanityfair.com/news/2010/10/the-vf-100-201010.

Dixon, W. W. and G. A. Foster (2011) *21st-Century Hollywood: Movies in the Era of Transformation*, New Brunswick, NJ and London: Rutgers University Press.

Doherty, T. (2002), *Teenagers and Teenpics: The Juvenilization of American Movies in the 1950s*, Philadelphia, PA: Temple University Press.

Driscoll, C. (2011) *Teen Film: A Critical Introduction*, Oxford: Berg.

Ehrlich, M. (2006) *Journalism in the Movies*, Urbana and Chicago, IL: University of Illinois Press.

Fear, D. (2020) '"The Social Network" at 10: Fincher, Facebook and the Faking of an Empire', *Rolling Stone*, online, 1 October, https://www.rollingstone.com/feature/social-network-fincher-10th-anniversary-1042538/.

Fisher, A. (2018) *Valley of Genius: The Uncensored History of Silicon Valley, as Told by the Hackers, Founders and Freaks Who Made It Boom*, New York, NY and Boston, MA: Twelve.

Fisher, M. (2009) *Capitalist Realism: Is There No Alternative?* Ropley: Zero Books.

Fisher, M. (2012) 'Precarious Dystopias: *The Hunger Games*', *Film Quarterly*, Vol. 65, No. 4, pp. 27–33.

Flynn, G. (2012) *Gone Girl*, London: Phoenix.

Frame, G. (2014) *The American President in Film and Television: Myth, Politics and Representation*, Bern: Peter Lang.

Garber, M. (2019) 'One Way *The Social Network* Got Facebook Right', *Atlantic*, online, 3 February, https://www.theatlantic.com/entertainment/archive/2019/02/one-way-social-network-got-facebook-right/581908/.

Gladwell, M. (2000) *The Tipping Point: How Little Things Can Make a Big Difference*, London: Little, Brown.

Gladwell, M. (2008) *Outliers: A Story of Success*, London: Penguin.

Gladwell, M. (2019) *Talking to Strangers*, London: Penguin.

Goi, L. (2018) 'Close-Up on "The Social Network"', *Notebook*, online, 5 June, https://mubi.com/notebook/posts/close-up-on-the-social-network.

Grossman, L. (2010) 'The Making of the Facebook Movie: A TIME Roundtable', *Time*, online, 23 September, http://content.time.com/time/magazine/article/0,9171,2021066,00.html.

Harari, N. Y. (2015) *Homo Deus: A Brief History of Tomorrow*, London: Vintage.

Harris, M. (2010) 'Inventing Facebook', *New York*, online, 17 September, https://nymag.com/movies/features/68319/#print.

Harris, P. (2009) 'A Sexy Saga of Facebook's Birth – But Is It Fantasy?', *Guardian*, online, 5 July, https://www.theguardian.com/books/2009/jul/05/facebook-accidental-billionaires-zuckerberg.

Heller, N. (2010) 'You Can't Handle the Veritas', *Slate*, online, 30 September, https://slate.com/news-and-politics/2010/10/what-the-social-network-gets-wrong-about-harvard-and-facebook.html.

Isaacson, W. (2011) *Steve Jobs*, London: Little, Brown.

James, N. (2010) '2010: The Year in Review – Introduction', *Sight & Sound*, Vol. 21, No. 1, online, http://old.bfi.org.uk/sightandsound/polls/films-of-2010-intro.php.

Johnson, S. (2005) *Everything Bad Is Good for You: Why Popular Culture Is Making Us Smarter*, London: Penguin.

Jones, K. (2010), 'Only Connect', *Sight & Sound*, Vol. 20, No. 11, pp. 34–36.

Kahnemann, D. (2011) *Thinking, Fast and Slow*, London: Penguin.

Kaklamanidou, B. (2018) *Easy A: The End of the High-School Teen Comedy?* Abingdon and New York, NY: Routledge.

Kamenetz, A. (2006) *Generation Debt: Why Now Is a Terrible Time to Be Young*, New York, NY: Riverhead Books.

Karim, A. (2020) 'Ten Years Later, Author Ben Mezrich on the Book behind "The Social Network"', *Forbes*, online, 18 October, https://www.forbes.com/sites/anharkarim/2020/10/18/10-years-later-author-ben-mezrich-on-the-book-behind-the-social-network/?sh=6d8f62361ebd.

Kasman, D. (2010) 'David Fincher and the Sad Facts', *Notebook*, online, 1 October, https://mubi.com/notebook/posts/david-fincher-and-the-sad-facts.

Kendall, T. (2016) 'Staying on, or Getting Off (the Bus): Approaching Speed in Cinema and Media Studies', *Cinema Journal*, Vol. 55, No. 2, pp. 112–118.

King, G. (2009) *Indiewood, USA: Where Hollywood Meets Independent Cinema*, London and New York, NY: Bloomsbury.

Kirkpatrick, D. (2010a) *The Facebook Effect: The Real Inside Story of Mark Zuckerberg and the World's Fastest-Growing Company*, London: Virgin Books.

Kirkpatrick, D. (2010b) 'With a Little Help from His Friends', *Vanity Fair*, online, 6 September, https://www.vanityfair.com/culture/2010/10/sean-parker-201010.

Kois, D. (2008) 'The Aaron Sorkin Facebook Movie: A Facebook History', *New York*, online, 28 August, https://www.vulture.com/2008/08/the_aaron_sorkin_facebook_movi.html.

Kozloff, S. (1988) *Invisible Storytellers: Voice-Over Narration in American Fiction Film*, Berkeley and Los Angeles, CA and London: University of California Press.

Lepore, J. (2021) 'Facebook's Broken Vows', *New Yorker*, online, 26 July, https://www.newyorker.com/magazine/2021/08/02/facebooks-broken-vows.

Leskowitz, A. R. (2010) 'Ambition and Obsession Drive Fincher's Flawless "Social Network"', *Harvard Crimson*, online, 30 September, https://www.thecrimson.com/article/2010/9/30/zuckerberg-facebook-social-movie/.

Levy, S. (2020) *Facebook: The Inside Story*, London: Penguin Business.

Lewis, J. (1992) *The Road to Romance & Ruin: Teen Films and Youth Culture*, Abingdon and New York, NY: Routledge.

Lewis, M. (2003) *Moneyball: The Art of Winning an Unfair Game*, New York, NY: W.W. Norton and Company.

McGuigan, J. (2009) *Cool Capitalism*, London: Pluto Press.

McKee, R. (1998) *Story: Substance, Structure, Style and the Principles of Screenwriting*, London: Methuen.

Manovich, L. (2001) *The Language of New Media*, Cambridge: MIT Press.

Manovich, L. (2002) 'What Is Digital Cinema', in N. Mirzoeff (ed) *The Visual Culture Reader*, 2nd edition, London and New York, NY: Routledge, pp. 405–416.

Maslin, J. (2009) 'Harvard Pals Grow Rich: Chronicling Facebook without Face Time', *New York Times*, online, 19 July, https://www.nytimes.com/2009/07/20/books/20maslin.html.

Mezrich, B. (2002) *Bringing Down the House: The Inside Story of Six MIT Students Who Took Vegas for Millions*, New York: The Free Press.

Mezrich, B. (2009) *The Accidental Billionaires*, London: Arrow Books.

Murch, W. (2001) *In the Blink of an Eye: A Perspective on Film Editing*, Los Angeles, CA: Silman-James Press.

Nelson, E. H. (2017) 'The New Face of an Old Genre: The Franchise Teen Film as Industry Strategy', *Cinema Journal*, Vol. 57, No. 1, pp. 125–133.

Phillips, M. (2020) '"The Social Network" 10 Years Later: A Grim Online Life Foretold', *New York Times*, online, 5 October, https://www.nytimes.com/2020/10/05/movies/the-social-network-facebook.html.

Purse, L. (2016) 'Affective Trajectories: Locating Diegetic Velocity in the Cinema Experience', *Screen*, Vol. 55, No. 2, pp. 151–157.

Robards, B. and S. Lincoln (2020) *Growing Up on Facebook*, New York: Peter Lang.

Saraiya, S. (2020) '*The Social Network* Got Facebook and Zuckerberg All Wrong', *Vanity Fair*, online, 6 October, https://www.vanityfair.com/hollywood/2020/10/the-social-network-got-facebook-and-zuckerberg-all-wrong.

Schreiber, M. (2016) 'Tiny Life: Technology and Masculinity in the Films of David Fincher', *Journal of Film and Video*, Vol. 68, No. 1, pp. 3–18.

Shary, T. (2002) *Generation Multiplex: The Image of Youth in American Cinema*, Austin, TX: Texas University Press.

Shary, T. (2005) *Teen Movies: American Youth on Screen*, London and New York: Wallflower Press.

Shary, T. and A. Seibel (eds) (2007) *Youth Culture in Global Cinema*, Austin, TX: University of Texas Press.

Shaviro, S. (2010) *Post-Cinematic Affect*, Winchester: Zero Books.

Sheehan, R. (2013) 'Facebooking the Present: The Biopic and Cultural Instantaneity', in T. Brown and B. Vidal (eds) *The Biopic in Contemporary Film Culture*, New York, NY and Abingdon: Routledge, pp. 35–51.

Smith, Z. (2010) 'Generation Why?' *New York Review*, online, 25 November, https://www.nytimes.com/2020/10/05/movies/the-social-network-facebook.html.

Solomon, B. (2012) 'Eduardo Saverin's Net Worth Publicly Revealed: More Than $2 Billion In Facebook Alone', *Forbes*, online, 18 May, https://www.forbes.com/sites/briansolomon/2012/05/18/eduardo-saverins-net-worth-publicly-revealed-more-than-2-billion-in-facebook-alone/?sh=2f6d12a232ac.

Sonnet, E. (1999) 'From *Emma* to *Clueless*: Taste, Pleasure and the Scene of History', in D. Cartmell and I. Whelehan (eds) *Adaptations: From Text to Screen, Screen to Text*, London and New York, NY: Routledge, pp. 51–62.

Sorkin, A. (2019) 'Aaron Sorkin: An Open Letter to Mark Zuckerberg', *New York Times*, online, 31 October, https://www.nytimes.com/2019/10/31/opinion/aaron-sorkin-mark-zuckerberg-facebook.html.

Tiffany, K. (2017) 'In 2010 The Social Network Was Searing – Now It Looks Quaint', *The Verge*, online, 17 March, https://www.theverge.com/2017/3/17/14946570/the-social-network-facebook-mark-zuckerberg-president-of-the-world.

Trumbore, D. (2020) 'How David Fincher's Early Commercial Work Paved the Way for His Hollywood Success', *Collider*, online, 2 December, https://collider.com/david-fincher-commercials-explained/.

Tucker, A. (2014) *Interfacing with the Internet in Popular Cinema*, New York: Palgrave Macmillan.

Vargas, J. A. (2010) 'The Face of Facebook', *New Yorker*, online, 13 September, https://www.newyorker.com/magazine/2010/09/20/the-face-of-facebook.

Vernallis, C. (2004) *Experiencing Music Video: Aesthetics and Cultural Context*, New York, NY: Columbia University Press.

Wyatt, J. (1994) *High Concept: Movies and Marketing in Hollywood*, Austin, TX: University of Texas Press.

Index

For Product Safety Concerns and Information please contact our EU
representative GPSR@taylorandfrancis.com
Taylor & Francis Verlag GmbH, Kaufingerstraße 24, 80331 München, Germany